# CULTURE IS THE CURRICULUM

## THE BLUEPRINT FOR FRAMEWORKS, SCRIPTS & STRATEGIES THAT FINALLY MAKE YOUTH ENGAGEMENT EFFECTIVE

BY:
K-RAHN VALLATINE

CULTURE IS THE CURRICULUM

*THE BLUEPRINT FOR FRAMEWORKS, SCRIPTS & STRATEGIES THAT FINALLY MAKE YOUTH ENGAGEMENT EFFECTIVE*

545 N. Rimsdale Ave #1716
Covina, CA 91722



Book Design by HMDPublishing.com
Cover Design by K-Rahn Vallatine & Virtually Possible Designs

The author is available for keynotes, trainings and workshops
support@innersunconsulting.com
ISBN: 979-8-9946924-0-0

# CONTENTS

# INTRODUCTION

## *The Day I Realized Compliance Wasn't Success*

There's an invisible ceiling over every young person you serve—and most of them don't even know it's there.

I didn't see it at first either.

I was standing face-to-face with a young man who had every reason to hate the world. He was angry, tattooed up, jaw clenched tight, pacing like a storm was brewing inside his chest. We were in a juvenile detention center. Pale concrete walls. Heavy doors. That institutional buzz of flickering lights overhead.

This wasn't my first time walking into a unit like this—in fact, it was my everyday work environment.

The young man's eyes were glazed with confusion and frustration. One wrong word, one wrong move... and I knew we were seconds from some type of physical altercation or meltdown he couldn't easily come back from.

I had this knot in my stomach. That feeling.

*"What do I even say that won't set him off?"*
*"How do I help when nothing seems to matter anymore?"*

*"Am I really making a difference—or just collecting a paycheck in a broken system?"*

I knew what the textbooks might say. I knew what the staff handbook would suggest.

But in that moment, none of it felt real. None of it felt human.

I didn't need a script.
I needed a way.

Instead of repeating the outdated script I was taught in our last out-of-touch staff training—you know, the one that tells you to "redirect the behavior" and "stay neutral" like we're all emotionless robots—

I decided to simply say:

"Yo, you good?"

He looked at me like no one had asked him that in years.

Not "What's wrong with you?"
Not "Calm down or I'm writing you up."

Just a real, human question.

He didn't answer right away.

But the tension in his shoulders dropped a little. His eyes shifted—not softened, but *seen*.

And in that small pause, something changed.

That moment wasn't magic.
It wasn't clinical.
It was connection.

And that moment became the first crack in the wall between us.

See, I didn't start off this work as *an expert*. I started as a kid who *was* that young man.

Disengaged. Angry. Wearing the mask.

I didn't read about this work from a safe distance—I *lived* it.

No, I was not incarcerated by the prison system. Instead, I was incarcerated by a skewed self-identity, a limited mindset, and poor self-worth that led me to make unhealthy decisions and engage in my own self-sabotage.

I lived under an invisible ceiling I didn't even know was there.

And the story I believed about myself—*"You're not enough. You're behind. You don't belong."*—became the boundary I couldn't break through.

Not because I didn't have opportunity.
Not because I didn't have people who cared.

But because the ceiling wasn't built by my circumstances. It was built by what I came to believe about myself because of my circumstances.

So when I started working with youth professionally, I understood the code. The silence. The shame. The fear.

I knew how connection could literally mean the difference between life and death in some environments.

I entered this work thinking that deep understanding—my passion, presence, and lived experience—would be enough.

And for a while, it looked like it was.

The kids respected me. I got them, and they got me. Staff would say, *"You have a gift."* Youth would say, *"You're different."*

I was the one who could calm the tension in the room. The one who "got through."

And I believed that charisma and sincere care would carry me.

But slowly, I started seeing cracks.

Yeah, they listened to me...
But they weren't changing.

They complied when I was in the room.
But when I left?

Same fights.
Same disrespect.
Same recidivism.

It started to wear on me. Month after month...I was burning out. Running on autopilot. Disconnected from the same youth I once felt a deep kinship with.

And worst of all?

I started questioning if I was still a part of the solution—or was I now just part of the machine?

Not transforming lives. Just helping the system run smoother.

That's when it hit me. We were all stuck in the old model. Trying to control behavior instead of understanding it. Rewarding compliance instead of developing character. Pushing rules and routines while ignoring pain and purpose. We had created a paradigm where a "good day" was just a day with no incidents, no paperwork, no calls from the supervisor.

We weren't aiming for transformation.
We were just trying to survive the shift.

And I realized...

The youth weren't the only ones in survival mode—we were, too.

Staff were emotionally exhausted. Morale was low. Turnover was high. People were walking around numb. And all the passion in the world couldn't patch the cracks in the foundation.

That's when I knew something had to change.

I wasn't okay with just "keeping the peace" anymore. I didn't want to be part of a system that trained youth to be quiet—but not whole.

So I made a decision: I was going to figure out how I could make a deeper, lasting impact.

And not just for the youth—but for the staff, too.

I didn't enroll in a PhD program. I didn't wait for permission. I dug in and got straight to work.

I consumed everything I could to learn more about culture, success, and human behavior.

Then one day, I was invited to enroll in a 4-part community training with Dr. Brenda Ingram—a subject matter expert on psychological and emotional trauma. I had never heard of trauma at the time, so I was totally intrigued by the information she presented.

As she spoke about the frontal lobe and dysregulation, I thought about the youth I worked with. As she continued and spoke about the amygdala being an internal alarm system, I thought about *myself*. Then she said something that flipped my whole world:

"The question isn't 'What's wrong with you?'
It's 'What happened to you?'"

That hit like a Mike Tyson body blow.

After this training I dug even deeper:

Books. Interviews. Peer-reviewed research. University lectures. Staff trainings.

I studied the brain—how the amygdala triggers our internal alarm system. I studied emotional regulation, educational equity, child development, family systems. I dissected theories from psychology, education, and neuroscience—

And I filtered all of it through one question:

"Does this make sense in real life with real youth in real systems?" And slowly, a new lens began to form. A lens that didn't just explain behavior—but honored the human connection and human experience.

Because suddenly, all those angry outbursts I used to try to control...
I now saw as *communication*.

They weren't problems.
They were protection.

Defense mechanisms for kids who didn't feel safe. And in that moment, I realized something even deeper: The invisible ceiling wasn't just built by trauma. It was built by the story trauma told them about who they were.

*"You're damaged."*
*"You're broken."*
*"You're the problem."*

And once that story became their identity, it didn't matter how many resources we gave them, how trauma-informed our approach was, or how many second chances we offered.

They would rise exactly to the height of that ceiling and no further.

Because here's the truth that nobody wants to say out loud:

Resources are the fuel.
Training is the vehicle.
Trauma-informed care is the repair shop.

But identity is the engine.

And if the engine is broken, nothing else moves.

Psychologists call it a self-fulfilling prophecy. Behavioral scientists call it psycho-cybernetics—built on the idea that no one operates beyond the boundary of their own self-image.

I call it the identity trap.

And it's the reason why so many well-meaning programs, interventions, and second chances fail. Not because the professionals aren't caring enough. Not because the resources aren't sufficient. But because we're treating the symptoms while the root cause—the story they believe about themselves—remains untouched.

Think about it:

You can teach a young person anger management techniques. But if they believe "I'm just an angry person," those techniques become a temporary fix at best. You can offer college prep classes. But if they believe "People like me don't go to college," they'll find a way to prove themselves right. You can pour love, mentorship, and opportunity into a young person's life. But if the voice in their head says, "I don't deserve this," they will self-sabotage—not because they're ungrateful, but because the behavior has to match the identity. And that's where most youth-serving systems get stuck.

We focus on behavior management. Compliance. Consequences and rewards. Monitoring and accountability.

But compliance doesn't create transformation. It creates performance.

They learn to act the part while you're watching. They sign the contract. Sit through the program. Nod at all the right moments.

And the moment you turn around? They go right back to being who they believe they are.

Because you can't behavior-manage someone into a new identity.

Identity has to be inspired first.

And when it is—when a young person begins to see themselves differently, when the story shifts from "I'm the problem" to "I'm the solution," from "I'm at-risk" to "I'm the future"—everything changes.

The behavior follows naturally. Not because you forced it. But because it finally matches who they see themselves becoming.

That's not theory. That's psycho-cybernetics in action.

From that point forward, I stopped reacting to *what* youth did—

And started seeking *why*.

What happened next?

Everything changed.

Where I once avoided confrontation, I now met it with calm. Where I used to second-guess every word, I now led with clarity.

And the same young men who used to escalate, threaten, or shut down?

They understood I wasn't just resolving conflict—I was building loyalty. And that loyalty became transformation.

Years later, I found myself training professionals with Master's degrees.
PHDs.
System leaders.
People who wanted to understand how I was getting the results they couldn't.

But here's what I knew:
The magic wasn't in *me*.
It was in the model I had built—
A framework designed for real-life youth, real-time challenges, and real-world systems that were never designed with our realities in mind.

I called it the L.I.G.H.T. Model.

It was built for one purpose:
To replace behavior control with identity-based leadership.

Because behavior doesn't change until identity does.

See it's very tough to inspire identity transformation by accident. Many of us wing it and hope that one good conversation, one caring adult, or one powerful moment will be enough to rewrite years of internalized narratives.

But sustainable transformation requires a framework. Not a rigid, one-size-fits-all program. But a clear, intentional, repeatable process that *systematically* shifts identity while building the skills, healing the wounds, and creating the culture that makes that new identity stick.

Because without a framework, identity work becomes inconsistent. It depends too much on individual charisma, random moments of inspiration, or the right person being in the right place at the right time.

And when that person leaves? The transformation leaves with them.

That's why the framework matters.

But—and this is critical—the framework only works if it's designed to target identity first.

If your framework is built around behavior management, you'll get temporary compliance.
If your framework is built around skill-building alone, you'll get competence without confidence.

If your framework is built around trauma-informed care without identity transformation, you'll get healing without forward movement.

But when your framework is designed to learn a lens, inspire identity, guide growth, heal hurt, and teach tools—in that order—you get sustainable transformation.

You get young people who don't just *act* differently while you're watching.
You get young people who *see themselves* differently when no one's watching.

And that's when the ceiling shatters.

Not because you got lucky. Not because you found the one magical intervention.

But because you followed a framework intentionally designed to do what most systems seem to overlook:

Change the internal story. Inspire the identity. Transform the life.

That's not hope. That's strategy. And it's the only way to break through the invisible ceiling.

So that's why I wrote this book.

To help youth workers, educators, and mentors like you:

➡ Who care deeply, but feel drained.

➡ Who are tired of surface-level fixes.

➡ Who want to see transformation, not just temporary change.

This isn't theory.
It's the system that saved my work—and has transformed the lives of thousands.

If you've ever felt the weight of the work...
If you've ever wondered if your passion is enough...
If you've ever wanted to be more than just another staff member...

Then keep reading.

Because the next few pages might just remind you why you started in the first place—
And more importantly,
show you how to finish strong.

This isn't just a book you read once and put on the shelf. It's a resource you'll return to again and again. Inside, you'll find:

➡ Key insights that shift how you see youth behavior

➡ Real-world scripts to de-escalate, engage, and connect

→ Activities that help shape identity and build trust

→ Strategies aligned with each pillar of the L.I.G.H.T. Model

Whether you're leading a classroom, running a reentry program, mentoring in the community, or managing a staff team—this book is designed to meet you where you are, and equip you with what works.

By the time you turn the last page, you won't just understand the "why" behind youth resistance... You'll have the "how" to unlock real buy-in and lasting transformation.

### *Access the Culture Reset Blueprint: A 50-Minute Executive Briefing*

# HOW TO USE THIS BOOK:

*Practical ways to apply the insights, tools, and scripts in real time*

This book isn't just something you read. It's something you use. If you're a youth worker, educator, mentor, counselor, or program director—this book was written for you. Whether you're brand new to the work or have years in the game, what you'll find in these pages is real, practical, and ready to go. Here's how to get the most out of it:

## 1. Read for the Shift.

Each chapter will challenge the traditional way we've been trained to "manage" youth and offer a new lens rooted in emotional safety, identity, and real transformation. Read with an open mind and be willing to unlearn a few things.

## 2. Apply the Tools.

You'll find scripts, reflection questions, engagement strategies, and real-life scenarios throughout the book. Don't just skim them—use them. Try them with your team and with your students. In your next difficult moment. Small adjustments can lead to major breakthroughs.

## 3. Use It Like a Toolbox.

This book is designed so you can come back to it again and again. Struggling with burnout? There's a section for that. Need help inspiring identity in youth? Got you. Trying to guide your team through culture change? Let's do it.

## 4. Go Deep—Then Go Wide.

Once you've read and applied what's here, bring others along. Discuss it with your staff. Your colleagues. Your leadership. This book can serve as a launchpad for training, reflection, and culture change across your whole organization.

## 5. Let This Be the Beginning.

This book will give you the framework, the tools, and the mindset shift—But if you want to go deeper, faster, or system-wide...There are workshops, curriculum, training experiences, and coaching designed to help you bring the **L.I.G.H.T. Model** to your entire team or program. You don't have to figure it out alone.

Let's get into it. Because the work you do matters. And the way you show up to it...Might just change someone's life.

# A STORY YOU NEED TO HEAR BEFORE WE BEGIN:

## *The Kid Who Couldn't See Past The Ceiling*

Before we begin the first chapter of this book, I want to tell you a story. Not because it is dramatic — but because it is common. This is the kind of moment happening in youth programs every day,
and it reveals the invisible ceiling we must break.

Let me tell you about *Marcus*.

Marcus was 15 at the time. Bright kid. Quick wit. The kind of young man who could read a room in two seconds and tell you exactly what you wanted to hear. He'd been through three schools, two group homes, and more "intervention programs" than he could count. His file was thick. Trauma history. Behavioral incidents. Academic gaps. Every label you can imagine was in there: *At-risk. Oppositional. Defiant.* And Marcus? He wore those labels like armor.

When I asked him what he wanted to do with his life, he laughed. Not a happy laugh. A sarcastic one. "Man, people like me don't *do* anything but survive. That's it."

Fifteen years old. And the ceiling was already locked in place.

His teachers saw it too. They'd tried everything—behavior contracts, incentive programs, one-on-one check-ins. They gave him resources: tutoring, counseling, even a mentor from a local nonprofit. And Marcus would show up. He'd play the part. He'd say the right things, sign the papers, sit through the sessions. But nothing stuck. Because here's what nobody realized:

Marcus didn't believe he was *worth* the investment. Not because he was ungrateful. Not because he didn't care. But because every message he'd ever received—from the system, from his environment, from his family, from his entertainment, from the labels slapped on his file— told him the same story:

> *"You're the problem. You're broken. You're too far behind to ever catch up."*

And once that became his identity? The resources didn't matter. The trauma-informed approach didn't matter. The mentor didn't matter. Because the engine was broken.

One day, his mentor—a man named Derek who had grown up in the same neighborhood—sat down with Marcus and said something different.

He didn't ask him about his goals. He didn't lecture him about his behavior. He didn't try to motivate him with a pep talk about his "why."

Instead, Derek said this:

"Marcus, I don't see a problem when I look at you. I see a young man who's survived things most people couldn't.

And survival? That takes strength. Strategy. Intelligence. You've got all three. The question isn't whether you're capable. The question is: Who do *you* see when you look in the mirror?" Marcus didn't answer right away.

But Derek didn't leave it there. Because Derek understood something most people miss:

One powerful conversation doesn't rewrite years of internalized narrative. It's very tough to inspire identity transformation by accident, hoping that one good moment will be enough. Derek had a framework. And he followed it intentionally.

First, he helped Marcus <u>learn a new lens</u>.

Over the next few weeks, Derek didn't just tell Marcus he saw potential in him. He taught Marcus *how to see himself differently*. He walked him through his own story—not as a victim of circumstances, but as someone who had developed survival skills that could be redirected toward success.

He reframed Marcus's "defiance" as independence. His "anger" as passion that hadn't found a productive outlet yet. His "trust issues" as discernment that needed guidance, not suppression. Derek was teaching Marcus to see through a different lens. Not toxic positivity. Not ignoring the trauma. But reinterpreting the evidence.

Then, he began to <u>inspire a new identity</u>.

Derek started calling Marcus "the strategist." Not as a nickname. As an identity. He pointed out moments when Marcus displayed leadership, even in small ways—how he naturally looked out for younger kids in the program, how he could read social dynamics and navigate conflict, how he thought three steps ahead when most people only thought one.

Every time Marcus showed up, Derek reflected back the identity: *"That's what strategists do. That's who you are."*

And slowly—so slowly you could almost miss it—Marcus started testing that identity. He started asking himself: *What would a strategist do in this situation?*

The ceiling started to crack.

Next, Derek <u>guided Marcus's growth</u>.

Once the identity began to shift, Derek didn't just leave Marcus to figure it out on his own. He gave him structure. Small wins. Clear next steps.

He helped Marcus set goals that aligned with his new identity—not vague dreams, but concrete actions a "strategist" would take. Showing up on time. Completing assignments. Learning how to manage his emotions in high-pressure situations.

Derek wasn't managing Marcus's behavior. He was guiding his growth *from* the identity they were building together.

And because Marcus was beginning to see himself as a strategist, the behavior wasn't forced. It was natural. It *matched* who he was becoming.

Then, Derek helped Marcus <u>heal the hurt</u>.

Marcus had trauma. Real trauma. And Derek didn't skip over it or pretend it didn't matter.

But instead of making the trauma Marcus's identity, Derek helped him process it *in light of* his new identity.

*"What happened to you was real. And it shaped you. But it doesn't define you. You're not broken. You're a*

Derek connected Marcus with the right support—counseling, restorative practices, safe spaces to unpack the pain.

But the healing wasn't disconnected from the identity work. It was *integrated* into it.

Marcus wasn't healing to go back to who he was. He was healing to *become* who he was meant to be.

Finally, Derek <u>taught Marcus the tools</u>.

Once Marcus's identity was shifting, his growth was guided, and his healing was in motion, Derek equipped him with the practical tools he needed to sustain the transformation.

Communication skills. Conflict resolution. Financial literacy. How to advocate for himself. How to navigate systems that weren't built for him. And because those tools were being taught to a young man who now saw himself as a strategist—not a problem—Marcus absorbed them differently.

He wasn't learning because someone made him. He was learning because it *aligned* with who he believed he was becoming.

By the end of that year, Marcus wasn't just attending school—he was mentoring younger kids in the program.

He wasn't just completing assignments—he was asking for more.

He wasn't just surviving—he was *building*.

What changed?

Not the resources. Those were always there.

Not the trauma-informed care. That was in place from day one.

Not even Derek's care and commitment—plenty of people had cared about Marcus before.

What changed was that Derek had a framework.

A clear, intentional, repeatable process designed to do one thing:

Inspire identity first. Then guide everything else from there.

**Learn the lens.**
**Inspire the identity.**
**Guide the growth.**
**Heal the hurt.**
**Teach the tools.**

That's not luck. That's not magic. That's not hoping the right person shows up at the right time.

That's the L.I.G.H.T. Model.

And it's the reason Marcus didn't just have one good moment. He had a *sustainable transformation*.

Because when you have a framework designed to shatter the invisible ceiling, you don't just change behavior. You change identity. And when you change identity, you change everything.

That's the invisible ceiling.

And that's why your resources, your training, and your trauma-informed approach will only go as far as the identity allows.

But when you pair them with a framework intentionally designed to inspire identity transformation?

That's when the ceiling shatters.

That's when transformation becomes inevitable.

That's when young people don't just survive—they build.

# CHAPTER 1

# DECODING "AT-RISK"

## *Why Behavior Isn't the Problem— Your Lens Is*

Let me ask you a question that might seem rhetorical at first: Do you work with "at-risk" youth?

If you're reading this book, I'm guessing your answer is yes. But before we go any further, let's slow that down for a second...

Because "at-risk youth" is one of those phrases we've all said so much, it's lost its original meaning. We say it in grant proposals.
In meetings. In behavior reports.
Sometimes even with pride—like, *"Yeah, I work with at-risk youth."* But what does it really mean?

Originally, when the term was coined back in the 1980s, it referred specifically to "youth at risk of academic failure." That was the whole definition.

But somewhere along the line, the meaning expanded... or maybe got diluted.

Because let's be honest—

Today, when most people hear "at-risk," what they *really* hear is:

→ Bad youth

→ Disengaged youth

→ Hard-to-reach youth

And just like that, we've stopped seeing the whole person. We've reduced them to a problem to be fixed—or worse, avoided.

So before you claim that title—"I work with at-risk youth"— it's important to ask yourself:

## At risk of *what?*

Because depending on the communities you serve and where you teach, your students and clients may be at risk of a whole lot more than low grades. They might be at risk of:

→ Incarceration

→ Hunger

→ Gang involvement

→ Domestic violence

→ Sex trafficking

→ Death

→ Poverty

→ Substance abuse

...and then they show up in your classroom or program
with a bad attitude—
and we're offended.

If I had to survive all those hurdles and pitfalls on a daily basis, and then sit in a desk and do algebra, with no context to how this information can enhance my current situation, I might have an attitude too.

This is why we have to challenge how we see them. Because if we keep using labels without understanding lives, we'll keep reacting to behavior instead of responding to pain.

"At-risk" doesn't describe that young man.
It doesn't define that young woman.

It describes the social factors they're forced to navigate through. And here's the part people forget: We're all at risk—depending on the risk factors. I say this in my trainings all the time:
*"Let my family go hungry for too long... and watch how 'at-risk' my mind becomes."*

Whether I act on it or not, my *mind* will start shifting. Survival mode doesn't care about credentials.

Let's be honest—as a youth professional I'm sure at some point you've said:

*"These kids just don't care."*
*"They're so hard to reach."*
*"You can't get through to them."*

And maybe you've felt that frustration more times than you care to admit.

You come in with a plan, a purpose, maybe even a lesson you *know* is solid...But the moment you try to connect?

Arms folded.
Eyes rolling.
Walls up.
Mouth shut.

You try redirecting, relating, reasoning, maybe even raising your voice.
And at some point, you walk out of the room wondering:

"Is it even worth it?"
"Do they even want help?"
"Am I the problem... or are they just broken?"

Here's what I want you to know up front:

Most of these young people are not simply hard-to-reach youth. Many are youth who've learned the world isn't safe. And often, we're just not speaking their language yet.

So when we talk about "at-risk," let's stop acting like we're talking about some *other*, isolated group. We're talking about people – human beings, who are reacting and behaving based on their experiences.

It's also extremely important to acknowledge that many of the people you interact with carry trauma. Notice I didn't say "many of the youth you work with." I said "the people."

Yes, that includes the youth.
But it also includes:

➜ Their parents

➜ Their communities

➜ Your colleagues

...and may even include *You!*

Think about it:

➜ Youth have experienced trauma

➜ Their parents likely have too, which affects how they parent

- → Your coworkers may carry trauma, which affects how they support or resist you
- → And yes, you may have unprocessed trauma that impacts how you see the world

That trauma shapes how a person shows up.
How they speak.
How they cope.
How they respond (or react).

So if we only focus on youth behavior without understanding the trauma in their ecosystem—
we're missing a very important piece of this puzzle we call youth engagement.

I wrote a book called "Beyond the Crack Generation: Surviving a Trauma Organized Culture." In the book I explain in great detail, through my own personal childhood journey, that much of the cultural norms found in gang and drug impacted communities are actually trauma responses. Meaning, in some areas, traumatic experiences are so common that we have created social norms in response or in anticipation to these traumatic experiences.

## What You See Isn't Always What's There

That eye roll you took as disrespect?
Might be a shield.

That silence you took as apathy?
Might be a coping mechanism.

That aggression you saw as defiance?
Might be a trauma response.

Behavior is communication.
And if we don't learn to read the language, we'll keep misinterpreting the message.

Here's the hard truth:

Most of the systems, policies, programs, and "best practices" we were handed…
weren't designed to support trauma-impacted youth *or* trauma-impacted professionals.

## The Real Problem? Our Lens Is Cracked.

Most of us were trained to respond to what youth *do*. But we weren't trained to understand *why* they do it. We were handed a script:

→   Set the rules

→   Maintain control

→   Enforce consequences

But the truth is…
Rules without relationship breed rebellion.
And control without connection leads to compliance, not commitment.

That's why this chapter—this whole book—starts with one essential idea:

Learn the Lens.

Before we rush to new strategies…
Before we jump into what to say or how to say it… We have to pause. And look again. With a different lens.

## Survival Mode Looks Different on Everyone

Some kids fight. Some shut down.
Some joke to deflect. Some get loud to avoid looking weak. But underneath all of that?

There's always a reason.

It might be:

- A history of being let down

- An environment that punishes vulnerability

- A learned belief that authority = danger

And if we don't adjust our lens, we'll keep trying to fix behaviors without ever addressing the root.

As I mentioned in the introduction, I've developed a transformative leadership development framework called the L.I.G.H.T. Model. The First Pillar is "Learn the Lens."

Before we teach a new curriculum...
Before we introduce a new rule system...
Before we even open our mouths...

We have to shift how we see.

Learning the lens means adopting a trauma-informed, emotionally intelligent mindset that helps us see beyond the behavior and into the *story*. Because when you shift how you see a young person— you shift how you engage them.
And when you shift how you engage them—
they shift how they show up.

## Try This: Lens Reflection Exercise

Think about the last youth who really got under your skin.
The one who frustrated you the most.
Picture their face. Picture the behavior.
Now ask yourself:

- What might they have experienced before they walked through my door?

- What might this behavior be protecting them from?

- What am I assuming about their attitude or ability?

→ What would change if I chose to see them through a lens of survival—not sabotage?

Write it down. Even better—talk about it with your team. The most powerful shift doesn't start with them. It starts with you.

**Key Takeaway:** Most youth aren't hard to reach.
They're tired of being misread.
And when you shift your lens—
you shift everything.

# RESOURCE SECTION

### *"Learn the Lens" in Action:*
### *Shifting from Reaction to Reflection*

It's one thing to shift your mindset.
It's another thing to shift how you respond—especially in the moment.

So, in this section, I'm giving you tools. Not theories. Real-world language, questions, and activities you can start using immediately to help yourself—and your team—begin seeing youth through a new lens.

## Section 1: Scripts That Shift the Lens

These are not magic words. They're mindset resets—phrases that help you interrupt the old habit of reacting to behavior and start connecting to the human behind it. Feel free to adjust the language at your professional discretion, to fit the culture of the population you serve.

### 1. When you feel disrespected:

Instead of saying: "You better fix your attitude."

Try: "I can tell something's bothering you. I'm down to talk or give you a minute if you need space."

**Why it works:** It shifts the tone from confrontation to curiosity. You're not backing down—you're backing up to see the full picture.

**When a student checks out:**

Instead of thinking: "If you don't care, then why are you even here?"

Try saying: "I notice you've been quiet lately. That's not like you. Are you good?"

**Why it works:** It replaces judgment with attention. It tells the youth, *"I see you, and I care enough to ask."*

**When a young person explodes emotionally:**

Instead of: "Calm down or leave."

Try saying: "There's probably more to this situation than what I'm seeing. Let's pause for minute. Help me understanding what's really going on."

**Why it works:** It names the intensity without escalating it. This gives space while holding boundaries.

**When you're feeling personally triggered:**

Say to yourself: "This isn't about me. This young person is probably projecting and taking out his/her feelings on me."

**Why it works:** It keeps you from personalizing their pain. That's how you stay present instead of reactive.

# Section 2: Real Examples of Lens Shifts in Action

## Case Example: Marcus, 15

**Old Lens:** Marcus is disrespectful. He rolls his eyes, talks back, and refuses to do assignments. "He's just lazy."

**New Lens:** Marcus is deeply insecure about his reading level and lashes out before someone can embarrass him. Behavior is his shield.

**New Approach:** Instead of calling him out, his teacher privately asked, "How can I support you in class without putting you on the spot?" Marcus didn't change overnight, but the tension dropped. He started turning in assignments more regularly. Not because he became a new person—
but because he finally felt safe enough to try.

## Case Example: Alana, 17

**Old Lens:** Alana skips school and shows no remorse. "She's just unmotivated."

**New Lens:** Alana is helping raise her siblings, works nights, and often doesn't sleep. Skipping isn't apathy—it's survival.

**New Approach:** Her counselor reframed expectations and created a flexible check-in system instead of defaulting to punishment. The result? Alana stayed in the program, and her attendance improved once her schedule aligned with her reality.

# Section 3: Group Discussion Topics

These questions can be used in staff meetings, professional development trainings, or small group debriefs.

Use them to spark meaningful reflection and challenge the old lens:

1. **What behavior in youth tends to trigger you the most—and why?**

2. **Have you ever misread a student's behavior, only to find out something deeper was going on? What shifted your view?**

3. **What social or cultural factors do your youth face that you didn't at their age? How might that affect how they show up?**

4. **What messages—spoken or unspoken—do your staff or systems send about "good behavior?" Are those messages healthy, or just convenient?**

## Section 4: Practical Activities to Help Shift the Lens

### The 3-Why Drill (Personal Reflection Tool)

Next time a student acts out, try this:

1. Ask yourself, *"Why did they do that?"*

2. Ask again, *"But why would that matter to them?"*

3. Then go one level deeper: *"What might they be protecting or proving?"*

This helps you slow down and move from reaction to reflection.

### The Survival Map Exercise (Team Activity)

On a whiteboard or chart paper, write the phrase:

"What risks do our youth face *before* they walk through our door?" Let the team call them out:

- → Violence

- → Hunger

- → Inconsistent parenting

- → Housing instability

- → Emotional neglect

- → Chronic stress

Then ask: "If *you* were navigating that... how would you show up in a classroom or program space?"

This helps humanize the behaviors we often label "disrespectful" and opens the door to empathy-driven engagement.

## From Behavior to Story: *Youth Engagement Activity*

**Use this prompt with youth:** "People see me as _______, but if they really knew me, they'd know _________."

Give them the chance to write, share, or just think about it. This creates safe space for identity-based conversation and helps youth see they are more than the labels placed on them.

## Final Word for This Chapter: Learning the lens isn't about letting go of structure.

It's about building a foundation that's strong enough to hold both truth and trust. When we stop labeling youth as problems—
and start seeing them as young people navigating problems— we unlock something bigger than behavior change. We unlock the beginning of real transformation. Next we'll move from how you see youth...to how you help them see themselves.

# CHAPTER 2

# Stop Managing Behavior. Start Shaping Identity.

## Why Compliance Isn't Enough—and What Real Buy-In Actually Looks Like

You've seen it before: The student who sits quietly in class. Follows the rules. Smiles at the right time. Nods when you speak. No issues. No attitude. No disruptions. But then a week later—he's caught fighting off campus. Gets arrested. Or disappears from the program altogether. And you're left wondering: "What happened? He was doing so well."

Let me break it to you gently: He wasn't doing well. He was just doing what he knew would keep him out of trouble.

### The Compliance Trap

This is the danger of focusing on behavior without touching identity: You create environments where youth learn how to act the part—but never learn how to *be* the part. We tell them to sit still, speak up, tuck in, fall in line. And if they do, we reward them. But inside, nothing has shifted. So, the moment they're in a new environment— one that doesn't offer structure or praise—they revert.

Not because they're "fake" or ungrateful...But because compliance was only a survival strategy.

Change is external.
Transformation is internal.

Change is about behavior.  Think of change as a caterpillar crawling to a new leaf to find food (behavior). Transformation is about identity. Think of transformation as the same caterpillar becoming the butterfly and flying to another field to find food (identity).

Change is, *"I know how to act right when you're watching."* Transformation is, *"I know who I am, so I act accordingly even when no one's watching."* That's the difference. And that's where identity comes in.

It was said by Canadian author Bob Proctor that "no one operates beyond the boundaries of their own self-image." Let that settle for a moment.

You may want to read that sentence again just to make sure you get it. Because for youth—and for us—it explains a lot. He goes to explain that the self-image is like a thermostat. If the thermostat in your classroom, your office, or your home is set to 72°, it doesn't matter what happens around it... that temperature is going to regulate itself.

If the room gets hotter than 72°, the A/C kicks on.
If it drops below 72°, the heater kicks in. Either way, the thermostat pulls the environment *back* to its programmed setting- 72°. Self-identity works the same way.

Whoever we believe we are—whoever we identify as— we'll find a way to act in alignment with that. Even if that means sabotaging something good.

Even if that means rejecting something that could change our life. That's why inspiring identity is non-negotiable when working with youth. If who they *think* they are doesn't match the opportunities in front of them, they'll reject the opportunity—just to stay consistent with their own identity. Let me show you what I mean.

## The Uniform Story

I was working with a young man—he had been incarcerated multiple times, and gang affiliation ran deep in his family.
His mother was gang affiliated.
His father had been gang affiliated—until he was murdered by gang violence.

And this young man?
He was deeply involved and "active."
He didn't just live in the culture—he *was* the culture.

But at some point, he wanted out.
He started seeking something different. He got a job at a popular coffee shop. Everything seemed to be going well...Until I got a call. "V..." he said—(that's what he called me, short for Mr. Vallatine).

"I don't know how long I can keep this job." I said, "Why not? What's going on?" He said, "The job is cool. The people are chill. The schedule is straight. But it's the uniform." I said, "What's wrong with the uniform?" He hesitated. Then he said it. "I don't feel like a crip when I wear that uniform."

That one sentence told me everything I needed to know. He wasn't rejecting the job. He was rejecting the identity conflict the job created inside him. Wearing that uniform didn't just make him feel different—it made him feel like he was *betraying who he thought he was*. I told him:

*"I know where you come from. I understand what you've been surrounded by. And I know how much you love your hood.*
*But let me tell you something...*
*You weren't born to be a crip.*
*That may have been your environment—but that's not your purpose."*

He went silent. Then he said, *"Man V... that's the realest thing anyone ever said to me."* Now, reading this, you might think—
*"That wasn't even that deep."* But to him?
It was like the clouds parted and God Himself dropped wisdom from the sky.

Why? Because everything around him—his family, his friends, his neighborhood, the culture—told him that gang life was his identity.

That it was his destiny.
His purpose.

And now, here comes this uniform, this job, this new path... And none of it matches the image he has of himself. He was ready to throw away the whole opportunity—not because he didn't want better—but because better didn't feel like *him*.

## Behavior Follows Belief

If a young man believes he's problem, he'll act like one. If a young woman believes she's only valuable when she's quiet and invisible, she'll play small to survive. If youth believe the only way to earn respect is through violence, then even the best afterschool program won't rewire that belief unless someone intentionally works to reshape how they see themselves. This is why the second pillar of the L.I.G.H.T. Model is Inspire Identity.

So, here's the real question: Who do your students think they are?

What identity are they committed to *preserving*, even if it means rejecting growth?

If a young man doesn't identify as a scholar,
then showing up to class consistently will feel like a betrayal. He'll find a way to act out, check out, or drop out—just to get back to who he believes he's supposed to be. If a young woman doesn't identify as a leader, she'll downplay her potential to stay in line with how others see her.
She'll pass the mic. Hide her brilliance. Shrink.

We've seen it too many times. And still we ask, *"Why don't they care about their grades?"*

Let me break it down another way. In my book *Beyond the Crack Generation*, I shared a story about a student who was failing almost every class. Math, English, History—you name it, he was flunking it. But put that same young man on a basketball court?

He transformed.

Every play mattered. Every point was life or death. One day he lost a game and yelled:
"Man, I *hate* losing!"

But when he got his report card with failing grades?
Nothing.
No emotion. No reaction.

Why? Because basketball was part of his identity. Academics weren't. He didn't see failing in math class as *losing.* He only saw *losing* as what happened when he didn't perform on the court.

## This Is Why Identity Comes Before Strategy

You can give youth all the tools in the world…
But if those tools don't align with how they see themselves, they'll drop them.

Compliance isn't the goal.
Transformation is.

And transformation begins with identity.

## Your Job Isn't Just to Keep Order. Your Job Is to Call Out Greatness.

When a youth says, *"I don't care,"* what they're often saying is, *"I don't believe I can be anything more."* When they say, *"Why should I try?"* they're really asking, *"Can you help me see myself in the shoes of success?"*

This is where your presence becomes powerful.

Not because you have all the answers, but because you're willing to speak to the version of them they can't yet see.

## Try This: Identity-Based Reflection Prompts (For Youth)

These can be journal prompts, group questions, or private conversations.

1. *What do people assume about you—and what's one thing they always get wrong?*
2. *If you could write your own definition of success, what would it be?*

3. *When do you feel most like yourself? Describe yourself in that moment?*

4. *"Who do you believe you are when nobody's watching?"*

5. *"What do you think you're known for?"*

6. *"What would change if you believed you were more than you think you are?"*

7. *"What's one label you've picked up—but you're ready to let go?"*

8. *If you were leading a program like this, what would you do differently?*

These questions don't fix behavior. They awaken belief. Because once a young person starts to question the old image—you can start planting a new one.

## Try This: Identity Scripts (For Adults to Say to Youth)

Use these statements to plant seeds:

➜ "I know where you come from—but I also see where you could go."

➜ "You've got a gift. You can play around with it, or you can build something with it."

➜ "You remind me of someone powerful. You just haven't stepped into it yet."

➜ "If you could see what I see in you, you'd stop settling for surviving."

You don't need a long speech. Just one sentence that makes them stop and think.

## Team Talk: How Is Our Program Shaping Identity?

Ask your team:

→ Are we only rewarding silence and compliance—or are we reinforcing self-worth?

→ Do our rules reflect adult convenience or youth growth?

→ Are we providing mirrors—or just manuals?

Because the truth is:

Youth don't rise to programs.
They rise to belief.

When you stop trying to *manage behavior* and start *shaping identity,*
you unlock more than engagement—
you unlock possibility.

And that's what we're here to do.

Your job isn't just to change how they act.
It's to change how they see themselves.

Because when identity shifts, behavior follows.
And when belief expands, so does the future.

# RESOURCE SECTION

*Identity in Action: Practical Tools to Inspire Self-Worth and Ownership*

## Staff Reminder: Before You Teach Identity—You Reflect It

How you show up speaks louder than anything you say. The tone of your voice, your energy, your expectations—those are all shaping identity in the room. So, before you ask youth to believe something new about themselves... check if you're modeling it.

Start here:

→ Do I speak to youth like they're a problem to manage or a possibility to nurture?

→ Am I reinforcing old labels ("lazy," "bad attitude," "hard-headed") with my reactions?

→ Do I recognize growth even when it's not perfect?

## Part 1: Identity-Based Scripts You Can Say Today

These are powerful one-liners that speak directly to identity. Use them in passing, one-on-one, or during tough moments.

→ "You weren't born to just survive this system—you were built to shift it."

→ "You've got a gift. You just have to decide how to use it."

→ "You're more than the worst thing you've done."

→ "You've got leadership in you. I see it—even when you try to hide it."

→ "I don't care where you started. I care about where you decide to go."

> **Pro Tip:** Don't over-explain. Just drop the line and keep it moving. Let it *land*. Sometimes the seed needs silence to grow.

## Part 2: Identity-Building Questions (For Group or Journaling)

Use these prompts to spark reflection, conversation, or small group discussion.

### For Youth:

→ "If the world didn't label you, how would you introduce yourself?"

→ "What's something people get wrong about you?"

→ "If your life was a movie, what would the title be right now? What would the title of the sequel be?"

→ "What's one thing you've been through that makes you stronger?"

→ "What do you want to be known for one year from now?"

**For Staff:**

- ➜ "How does your own identity impact the way you lead youth?"
- ➜ "What unconscious labels have you placed on students—and are they helping or harming?"
- ➜ "What part of your story would shock your students if they knew it?"
- ➜ "Are you calling out greatness in youth—or just correcting behavior?"

## Part 3: Identity Reframe Activity (For Youth)

**Activity Name:** *"Who Do You Think You Are?"*

**Setup:** Give students two index cards.

**Card 1 Prompt:** *"Write three labels people have placed on you (positive or negative)."*

**Card 2 Prompt:** *"Now write three words YOU want to be known for."*

## Discussion Questions:

- ➜ "Which card has more power over your life right now?"
- ➜ "If it's Card 1, what would need to change for Card 2 to take the lead?"
- ➜ "Who are you surrounding yourself with that reinforces Card 1—or Card 2?"

This is a powerful tool for breaking old identities and claiming new ones.

# Part 4: The Mirror Exercise
# (For 1:1 or Small Group Use)

## Prompt:

"What would you say to a younger version of yourself if they were going through what you're going through now?" Give time to write, reflect, or speak out loud.

## Why it works:
It shifts youth out of survival and into self-reflection and self-compassion—key elements of identity development.

# Part 5: Identity Alignment Check
# (For Staff to Use with Programs)

Use this as a quick internal audit with your team.

Ask:

→ "Does our reward system honor identity growth—or just obedience?"

→ "Are we reinforcing rules or reinforcing self-worth?"

→ "Are we hiring and training people who can model strong identity—not just manage youth behavior?"

→ "What's one policy, phrase, or practice we use that might be clashing with the identity we're trying to build?"

This helps ensure that your program culture isn't silently contradicting the outcomes you say you want.

# Part 6: Identity Shift Tracker
# (Daily Practice Tool)

Encourage staff or youth to track this weekly:

| Day | Moment I felt out of alignment with who I want to be | What I did next | One thing I'll do differently tomorrow |
| --- | --- | --- | --- |
| Mon | | | |
| Tue | | | |
| Wed | | | |
| Thurs | | | |
| Fri | | | |

This builds self-awareness and ownership—both essential ingredients for identity-based transformation.

## Closing Thought:

Behavior doesn't shift until belief does.
And belief doesn't shift until identity is addressed.

If you want real buy-in, you have to help youth see themselves as more than what they've survived.

More than what they've been told.
More than what they used to believe.

Inspire them—and you'll see the rest begin to fall into place.

# CHAPTER 3

# DON'T JUST INSPIRE THEM— DEVELOP THEM.

## *How to Turn Buy-In Into Breakthrough Using Future Identity as a Compass*

You ever worked with a young person who got hyped up in your session? —they were locked in, focused, nodding their head like *"Yeah, this is it"*...But two days later they ghosted you?

Missed their check-in?
Got caught doing the very thing they said they were done with?

It'll leave you standing there like, *"Wait... what just happened?"* They were *just* talking about turning their life around.
They said they wanted more.
Yeah. That moment hurts.

But let me be clear:

Inspiration isn't enough.
If it doesn't turn into growth, it'll fade.

You can light a fire in someone's heart,
but if you don't teach them how to feed it—
that flame will fade every time the wind blows too hard.

That's why the third pillar of the L.I.G.H.T. Model is Guide the Growth.

Because youth don't just need to be seen or validated—
they need to be developed.

Sometimes we confuse "getting it" with *being ready to live it.* Just because a young person agrees with your advice doesn't mean they're ready to apply it consistently.

Not because they're playing games—
but because growth takes support.

It takes practice.
Mistakes.
Re-do's.
And someone patient enough to walk with them through it.

See, this chapter is about what happens *after* the "Aha."
After the buy-in.
After the breakthrough.

What do you do when a young person sees who they could be—
but keeps falling back into who they've always been?

That's when they need a compass.

Something to guide their next move.
Something to remind them of who they're *becoming*—not just who they've been.

That compass is what I call *future identity*.

In the last chapter I said self-Image is a thermostat. In this chapter we'll discuss how future identity is a compass.

Remember, "No one operates beyond the boundaries of their own self-image."

You can put a young person in a new environment, give them new clothes,
a new mentor, a new opportunity...

But if their self-identity hasn't changed,
they'll find a way to pull themselves back to who they believe they are.

That's why development has to be intentional.
It's not just about getting youth to behave or believe in the moment—
It's about guiding them to build the *internal compass* that leads their behavior in the future.

## Story: Vernon and the Fight

I remember being invited to speak at an alternative school—a Community Day school for students who had been expelled from the school district.

I was there to do professional development with the staff and visit classrooms to talk with the students.

After the training, the principal pulled me aside.
He told me, *"There's one student I really want you to meet."*

For confidentiality purposes, we'll call him "Vernon." He told me Vernon was charismatic.
Bright.
A natural leader.

But distracted.
Inconsistent.
Always finding himself in trouble.

He said, *"I really believe in this kid. He just needs some-one to speak life into him."*

So as the morning went on, I made my way through the classes, and eventually, I made it to Vernon's class.

I quickly observed that the principal was right—
the young brotha had presence.
Confident. Funny.
Everyone in the class seemed to follow his lead.

After I spoke to the class and the class ended, Vernon stuck around to talk to me.
He said, *"Mr. Vallatine... I wanna do what you do. I wanna help the youth. The youth need guidance."*

I can't lie, that made me laugh a little—
he's 17, talking about "the youth" like he's 45.

I held my chuckle in because I saw he was serious, and I knew what he meant.
He saw a future version of himself that made sense to him. And that's what mattered. For all I knew, at age 17, he may have already lived the life of a 45-year old. I told him, *"That's real. Keep doing the work. Stay focused. You've got a story that could help people one day."*

I shook his hand and we exchanged smiles. It was a good moment.

About an hour later, I was sitting outside during the school's lunch period, in a quiet spot on campus. All of a sudden I saw many students running in one direction.

If you know, like I know that only means two things. And I didn't hear gunshots… so that left one option: it had to be a fight.

I watched from a distance as security rushed over.
Students scattered.
To my surprise, in the middle of the crowd—shirt off, yelling, fists clenched—was my junior youth counselor Vernon.

Yep. He was the one fighting.

They calmed him down and escorted him into the office. A few moments later, the principal walked up to me and said, *"Do you mind talking to him?"*

I said, "Sure."
But to be honest—I didn't know what to say.

I had just met the kid an hour ago.
I didn't have a speech planned.
I didn't have a magic line.

But I walked into the office ready to support where I could. Vernon was sitting there alone, while all of the staff sat in the next office. His were fists balled up. His jaws were clenched. He was still breathing heavy.

I sat down beside him quietly.
No script.
No sermon.

Just silence. Then I looked at him… and said two words: "You straight?"

He looked down at his hands—knuckles swollen, bruised, still bleeding.

He didn't answer.

As we sat in silence he finally said, "Yeah… I'm good." A few more seconds of silence passed.

Then he said: "I'm sorry you had to see me like that. But you know these dudes be tripping."

I told him: "No judgment here. I know how fast things happen.

But remember, you have a calling to help the youth. And if that's who you're becoming, then every choice you make now needs to reflect that.

This fight? This doesn't define you.
But the next decision you make—that's what will build you.
You've got another chance tomorrow. Don't waste it."

## Future Identity Is the Compass

What I did in that moment wasn't complicated.
I just reminded Vernon of who he *said* he wanted to be.
And used that future identity as his compass for today.

That's how you *guide growth*.

When youth see something better,
you have to keep naming it, pointing back to it,
and using it as the reference point for every
conversation.

## The Real Role of a Mentor

If you're in this work, you're not just a staff member.
You're a growth guide.
You're a blueprint-holder.
You're a walking example of *what's possible on the other side.*

Not perfect.
Not above them.
But a few steps ahead—
willing to say, *"Come this way. I've been there."*

Your job isn't to carry them.
It's to walk with them until they learn to carry themselves.

## Why Growth Feels Slow (But Isn't)

Let's break something right now:
Progress won't always be linear.

Just because they had a good week doesn't mean they're "delivered."
Just because they had a bad day doesn't mean they failed.

This is important:
When you're guiding someone through growth,
you have to celebrate the effort—not just outcomes.

Look for:

→ The moment they paused before reacting

→ The first time they asked for help

→ The day they returned after messing up

→ The decision to be honest when it would've been easier to lie

These are real wins—even if they don't fit neatly in a data report.

So when a student gets off track, ask them:

→ "Is that how a future business owner moves?"

→ "Would a college-bound student make that decision?"

→ "Does this action match who you're becoming?"

→ "You told me you want to go pro—what would the best version of you do right now?"

You're not lecturing. You're re-centering them.

That's development.

## Development Means Teaching Tools, Not Just Talking Goals

Goals sound good. But tools *get them there.*

Growth needs:

→ Time management

→ Emotional regulation

→ Boundary setting

→ Conflict resolution

→ Self-talk rewiring

→ Accountability practices

If we're not teaching these tools, we're just throwing motivational quotes at trauma.

Development takes time.
It's not just one talk.
It's not perfect.

But when you treat a young person like they're capable of growth—
they'll rise to the identity you reflect back to them. Not overnight.
Not without setbacks.
But with time, safety, and consistency—
they'll move.

Because growth doesn't just happen through pressure.
It happens through purpose.

## Try This: "What's Next?" Conversations

After a youth has a breakthrough moment or a big realization, don't just end the session. Ask:

→ "What's one small step you can take this week?"

→ "Who can you call when it gets hard?"

→ "What part of you is going to want to self-sabotage—and how can we prepare for that?"

→ "What does support look like for you right now?"

Don't just inspire them to feel.
Equip them to move.

## Try This: Growth Journaling Prompt

**Prompt:**

| *"This week I grew when I…"* |
| *"I messed up when I…"* |
| *"Next time I will…"* |

Have them track this weekly—keep it low-pressure. It builds self-awareness, accountability, and forward motion.

## Try This: "Show Me You Heard Me" Strategy

After a 1:1 session or group lesson, instead of asking, *"Did that make sense?"*

Say: *"Alright, show me how you're going to use that next time _____________ happens."*

This builds real-world application, not just head nods.

## Final Word:

Growth isn't always loud.
Sometimes it's invisible to the untrained eye.
But if you slow down, zoom in, and stick around—you'll see it. And more importantly…
they'll feel it. So don't just be a moment in their life. Be a part of their momentum.

Let's guide the growth.

# RESOURCE SECTION

*Guiding the Growth: Tools to Develop Identity-Driven Decision Making*

**Core Reminder:** Your job isn't just to motivate them. Your job is to help them anchor their daily decisions to the version of themselves they want to become. When the identity is clear, the choices become clearer.

## Part 1: Future Identity Scripts (Say These Out Loud)

Use these during redirection, conflict, goal setting, or daily conversations. The goal isn't to control—it's to *re-center* them on who they've told you they want to be.

**Reframing Poor Choices:**

→ "Is this how the version of you who wants to be free and successful moves?"

→ "You told me you want to be a leader—does this look like leadership?"

→ "I'm not mad at the mistake. I'm checking to see if you're still on track with who you said you were becoming."

## In Conflict or Post-Consequence Moments:

→ "This right here doesn't define you—but it can teach you if you let it."

→ "You've got a story you said you want to use one day. What chapter are you writing right now?"

→ "You don't owe me a better decision. You owe it to your future self."

## During Check-Ins:

→ "Who did you show up as today?"

→ "What would the 25-year-old version of you say about this choice?"

→ "Is today's decision going to make your future life easier—or harder?"

# Part 2: The Identity Alignment Tool (Group or 1-on-1 Exercise)

**Activity Name:** *"Who Am I Becoming?"*

**Step 1:** Ask the youth: "Who do you want to be in 2–5 years?" Let them be specific: NBA player, business owner, youth mentor, nurse, father, free man/woman, etc.

**Step 2:** Draw two columns.

| Choices I'm Making Now | Choices That Version of Me Would Make |
| --- | --- |
| Skipping school | Shows up every day |
| Fighting to save face | Solves problems without losing control |
| Getting high to cope | Finds new ways to release stress |

**Step 3:** Ask: "What's one thing you can change this week to close the gap between the two?"

This exercise builds self-accountability without shaming. You're not calling them out—you're helping them call *themselves* forward.

## Part 3: Growth Tracking Prompts (Use Weekly)

**Goal:** Build a rhythm of reflection and decision-making based on who they want to become.

You can use these as journal prompts, check-in forms, or verbal conversation starters.

### Weekly Questions:

→ "What's one decision I made this week that aligned with my future identity?"

→ "What's one decision that pulled me away from it?"

→ "What's one thing I'll do different next week to stay on track?"

→ "Who can I call or check in with when I feel myself slipping?"

## Part 4: Staff Strategy Session

**Future Identity Circle:** Use this tool with your team or program staff to improve how you respond to setbacks and growth moments.

### As a staff, ask yourselves:

1. Do we know each youth's *future identity*—in their own words?

2.  Do we reference that identity consistently in conversations, redirections, and support?

3.  When a youth messes up, do we correct the behavior—or remind them who they are becoming?

4.  Are we rewarding quiet compliance, or celebrating identity-aligned progress?

## Part 5: Quick Tools for High-Impact Moments
## 30-Second Future Anchor (Quick Reset)

Say: "Pause. Real quick—who are you becoming again?"
"Good. Now let's act like it."

### 2-Minute Mirror Check

Ask: "Does this decision look like someone who's about
to _________?"
(Fill in with what they told you: "start their brand," "go D1,"
"stay out of jail," "become a mentor," etc.)

### When They Slip

Say: "This doesn't disqualify you.
But it does ask you a question:
Are you serious about the identity you said you wanted?"

Pause.
Let them answer.
Then move forward with them.

### Final Word:

You're not just helping youth stay out of trouble.
You're helping them stay in alignment.

That version of themselves they see—the one that's more
free, more focused, more fulfilled—

that's not a fantasy.
It's a blueprint.

Your job is to keep putting that blueprint in front of them
until they believe it's *real enough* to build.

CHAPTER 4:

# HEAL THE HURT

*Because it's hard to grow while guarding a wound.*

As youth service professionals, we all want better behavior from our kids— But what if the real issue isn't behavior?

What if what we're dealing with is unspoken pain that's showing up disguised as poor behavior?

That fight, that shutdown, that sarcasm...
may not be the real problem we should be focusing on "fixing"— these could very well be symptoms of something deeper - a wound that's finally speaking.

The world-changing abolitionist, Frederick Douglass once said:

*"It is easier to build strong children*
*than to repair broken men."*

Considering the rage, grief, flashbacks and internal wars he probably battled with daily as a man who was formerly enslaved, he knew firsthand about the effects of unhealed wounds.

These wounds may first show up as isolated *actions*, a random outburst, or meltdown. Over time, when not addressed, these isolated actions may show up on multiple occasions and is then considered a *behavior* or habit. As habits begin to set in, and the wound remains unaddressed they begin to fester and unfortunately now shows up as *character*. Once these wounds affect a person's character, it is now very difficult to get to the bottom or source of the issue. What once was an isolated problematic action, is now dominant characteristic of who they are!

A few years ago, I was working closely with a reentry organization, developing and facilitating trauma informed training and was invited to observe a class inside an adult men's correctional facility up in the Bay Area.

My main focus has always been youth—but I also do work with reentry (formerly incarcerated) populations. So, I took the flight and visited the jail. The minute I stepped into the classroom, it was clear this teacher "got *it*."

Her tone was calm.
Her spirit was warm.
And the classroom was structured.
You could feel the safety.

I sat quietly in the back, just watching as she delivered her lesson.

After she finished teaching her class, she gave her students an assignment. As the students quietly began working, one of the students—probably about 25 years old—sat off to the side, tossing a pencil in the air... catching it... and tossing it again.

Nothing aggressive, just... distant.

She walked over to him, smiled, and softly said,

"Hey, let's try to get some work done today, okay?" He gave a small nod. Then grabbed his pencil and wrote his name on his worksheet.

A little while later, she went back to him to check his work. But instead of seeing a completed worksheet, his paper was covered with a detailed drawing. She looked at it—genuinely impressed—and said, "Ohhh okay! You got some talent. You ever thought about joining an art class while you're in here? This is very good. But let's get this assignment done first, so I can give you credit for today."

She handed him a clean worksheet and moved on. No judgment. No drama. No scene. Just grace.

A few minutes later, he raised his hand and said:

"Ma'am... you know why I be messin' up in your class?" She tilted her head. "I wouldn't say you're messing up... but tell me."

He looked down, fidgeted with his pencil, then said: "It's cause I can't read too good."

Without batting an eye, she said, "Thank you for sharing that. Well you're in the right place to get the help you need. We'll work on that together."

Masterful!

I took a moment to process what I just witness unfold before my eyes - authentic trauma informed engagement. Then I raised my hand from the back of the class. "Yes Mr. Vallatine," she said.

I replied, "Do you mind if I ask your student something?" She nodded and said, "Sure, go ahead." I looked to him from the back of the class and asked: "Why'd you decide to tell her that right now?" He looked around the room. Looked down at his paper and said:

"Cause I don't care what nobody in here thinks about me." I gave a nod... and said "Ok. Solid. I was just curious." But inside, I was thinking:

Nah. It's more to it than that. It probably wasn't just that he didn't care.

It was probably that—for the first time—
He didn't feel like he had to protect the wound.

That classroom...was the first place in a long time where the pain didn't have to hide.

He'd clearly been carrying that reading challenge since childhood.
But that day?

That day was a breakthrough for him...he breathed a little easier.
That day, he left just a little more healed.

Remember, pain often wears a mask.

That mask might look like toughness. It might look like disengagement. Or silence. Or jokes. Or apathy. Or rage. But it's still a mask.

Too many of us youth professionals get overly distracted by the mask, and forget to ask:

"What is this young person *protecting*?"

Because every one of us—youth and staff alike—has had moments where we protected our pain with something else.

That student who "doesn't care" about school?

Maybe he cared once. Cared a lot.
But after enough failures, ridicule, or being overlooked—
not caring became the way he knew to survive and
protect himself.

That girl who gets into it with female staff constantly?
Maybe she's never had a safe woman in her life model boundaries without betrayal. Maybe this isn't an attack—maybe it's a test. "Can I trust you not to hurt me like the others did?" I'm sure you see where I'm going.

Until the hurt is healed, the growth is blocked.

## The Splinter Under the Skin

Imagine a splinter under your skin.

You bump it—it hurts. You touch it—it stings.
You leave it in too long—it gets infected.

Now imagine someone walks by and keeps poking it. Then they're confused when you flinch. When you snap. When you pull back.

That's what it's like trying to operate in the world with unhealed trauma. You react, not because you're defiant—But because you're defending the wound. And unfortunately, most systems don't ask "Where's the splinter?" They just get mad you're reacting to the pain.

Understand, this conversation is not about turning youth professionals into therapists.

But it is about refusing to be blind to the context of our work. And let's be clear, unhealed hurt doesn't just exist in the youth—
It lives in the staff, too. It's the educator who overreacts to disrespect because they've never healed from being disrespected in their own childhood home. It's the mentor who's "burnt out" but really just grieving the fact

that no matter how hard they try, the system keeps
chewing kids up. It's the counselor who shows up every
day but doesn't feel anymore.
Because compassion fatigue has set in and it's easier
to work on autopilot and check boxes than to feel
helpless and ineffective (If you've read my book "Beyond
the Crack Generation: Surviving a Trauma Organized
Culture" I give a personal example of this from my own
high school experience).

This work can be heavy. But healing isn't a luxury in this
line of work. It's a necessity.

## What We Don't Heal, We Transfer

If I don't heal my wounds, I'll bleed on kids who didn't cut
me. If I haven't made peace with my past, every time a
young person reminds me of "me at that age," I'll either try
to save them out of guilt—or punish them out of projection.

But what if we flipped that?

What if the pain was the portal?

What if our own healing made us better at creating healing spaces for them?

It's important to note here that we are not here to "save"
or "fix" our youth. We are here to help them heal, to give
them guidance and offer support. Having a *savior complex* can quickly lead to burn out and it can also lead
us to being judgmental. See, when I'm trying to save
you or fix you, I no longer see you, your path and your
circumstances. I only see where I'm trying to get you.
You become my project. And if you don't get to where
I'm trying to get you to, in the time I'm trying to get you
there, it's easy for resentment to build.

I like to think of myself as a light post planted on the path of the youth I encounter. I'm here to illuminate a healthy route and effective tools that can lead them and support them in getting to their desired destination.

# RESOURCE SECTION



## 1. Language That Responds to Pain, Not Just Behavior

Use these phrases when de-escalating, redirecting, or simply noticing something might be going on *beneath the surface.*

**Instead of:**

→ "What's wrong with you today?"
Try:

→ "Everything good today? I noticed you seem a little off."

→ "You don't have to talk about it, but I see you. I'm here if you need me."

**Instead of:**

→ "Fix your attitude."
Try:

→ "That doesn't sound like you. Wanna take a second to reset?"

→ "Let's slow it down. I'm listening and want to hear what you have to say."

## Instead of:

→ "Why are you always causing problems?"
Try:

→ "Help me understand what's really going on with you."

## Instead of:

→ "You're being disrespectful."
Try:

→ "Let's pause here. I want to make sure we both feel respected in this convo."

**Rule of thumb:** Don't assume pain is present—but *consider* that it might be. Speak to the person beneath the reaction, not just the reaction itself.

## 2. Trauma-Aware Classroom Norms

These ground rules center emotional safety without compromising structure.

### Healing-Centered Norms:

→ "We don't do embarrassment here. Correction is private, not public."
→ "We ask what happened, not what's wrong."
→ "We check in before we check out."
→ "We respect space—but we don't let silence replace support."
→ "You don't have to be perfect. You just have to keep showing up."

**Activity:** Invite your students to co-create the norms.

Ask: "What do you need to feel safe, respected, and seen in this space?"
Then post those norms up as *agreements*, not *rules*.

## 3. Self-Check: Burnout + Emotional Load Audit

This quick check-in can help youth professionals stay *self-aware and regulated.*

### Reflective Questions:

- Am I reacting to youth, or responding with awareness?

- Did anything today feel personal that probably wasn't?

- When was the last time I rested without guilt?

- What part of this job is hurting me right now—and have I named it?

- What used to make me love this work that I haven't done in a while?

**Quick Coaching Prompt:**
"Am I trying to save them... or support them? One leads to burnout. The other builds boundaries."

## 4. Scripts That Build Trust Without a Big Moment

You don't need a breakthrough to be consistent. Consistency is what builds the trust.

### Relationship-Building Scripts:

- "You good today? No pressure—just checking in."

- "You were on my mind yesterday. Wanted to tell you I see your effort lately."

→ "I'm not here to fix you. I'm just here to walk with you."

→ "You don't have to explain it all today. But when you're ready—I'm ready."

→ "That moment back there? I know it probably came from somewhere else. No judgment."

These phrases matter most when *nothing's wrong*. Trust is built between the breakdowns.

## 5. Activities for Culturally Responsive, Trauma-Informed Bonding

### "What I Carry" Journaling Exercise

Invite students to reflect silently or share aloud:

"If people really knew what I carry with me every day, they'd know..."

Follow with a creative prompt:
"I carry... (write a poem, draw an image, write a metaphor)."

### Debrief Questions:

→ How does carrying something heavy affect how we show up?

→ What does it look like to give someone grace—even if we don't know what they carry?

### "Mask / Mirror / Mentor" Visual Exercise

Create three boxes on a worksheet or whiteboard:

→ MASK – What do people see when I'm hurting but don't say anything?

→ MIRROR – What I see when I look at myself.

➔ MENTOR – The version of me I want to become—who's been through it and healed.

Use this activity to help students articulate pain, identity, and growth.

## Reflection Circle: "This Work Changed Me"

Invite your team to share in a non-judgmental circle:

➔ "What part of this work has changed me the most?"

➔ "What pain in me do I bring into this job—knowingly or unknowingly?"

➔ "Where do I still need healing to be fully present for the youth I serve?"

This activity builds staff vulnerability and collective resilience.

> **Final Reminder:** You don't have to be a therapist to *be therapeutic.* Just speak with intention, lead with awareness, and create the kind of emotional safety that makes healing possible.
>
> Because sometimes, the best intervention...isn't a lesson plan. It's a listening ear.

## Healing-Centered Language Swaps

*Speak to the person, not just the behavior.*

| Instead of Saying... | Try This Instead... |
| --- | --- |
| "What's wrong with you?" | "Everything good today? I noticed you seem a little off." |
| "Fix your attitude." | "That doesn't sound like the real you. Want to reset for a sec?" |

| | "Let's slow it down. You deserve to be heard and understood." |
|---|---|
| "Why are you always causing problems?" | "Help me understand—what's going on underneath this?" |
| "You're being disrespectful." | "Let's pause—I want to make sure we both feel respected in this convo." |
| | "You're bigger than this moment. Let's figure it out together." |
| "Don't act like that." | "You okay right now? I can tell something's coming up for you." |
| "You're being dramatic." | "I can tell this hit a nerve—let's talk it through when you're ready." |
| "You need to calm down." | "Let's breathe first, then figure out how to move forward." |
| "Stop crying. You're fine." | "Your feelings are valid—it's okay to feel this. Want a second to collect yourself?" |
| "If you don't like it, you can leave." | "You bring something real to this space. I want to make sure you feel seen here." |

**Pro Tip:** When unsure how to respond, try curiosity over control:

→ "What do you need right now to feel supported?"

→ "Want to step outside with me for a quick reset?"

→ "This doesn't feel like the full story—talk to me."

# CHAPTER 5

# TEACH THE TOOLS

*Because when the heart is ready, the right tool can change everything.*

**W**e often ask young people to do better.
Make better choices. Use their words. Think ahead. But we forget something fundamental:
A tool is only helpful when the hands holding it are ready. If a person's lens is still distorted, if their identity is still unstable, if they've never been taught how to grow or heal—then giving them tools is premature. It's not helpful—it's pressure. So, before we can teach the tools, we must first till the ground.

Once the lens is clear, the identity is seen, the growth is guided, and the hurt is being healed—*then* the tools can stick. Then they're not seen as a punishment or lecture. They're seen as empowerment. As keys. As strategy.

Because that's what this chapter is about:
How to stop reacting to behavior and start equipping for legacy.

Understand that the L.I.G.H.T. model is not just for the youth. As we talk about giving youth the tools they need to succeed, we must understand, tools are only effective

after transformation has begun.
And not just in the youth.
Also in us.

If the adult's lens is still distorted...
If identity isn't being inspired through our systems...
If growth is being forced instead of guided...If pain is being overlooked instead of healed...
Then we're not ready to hand over tools—We're handing over pressure. Pressure without preparation. Solutions without strategy.

This is why *Teach the Tools* is last in the L.I.G.H.T. Model.

Because by now, the professional is different.
The culture is different.
The expectations are different.

Now you're ready to use the tools.
Now you're ready to model them, reinforce them, and embody them.
Now you're not just teaching curriculum—you're building a climate.

## Carver and the Power of Culturally Rooted Tools

Let's take it back to the 1800s.

To a man named George Washington Carver—born enslaved, orphaned, and yet one of the greatest agricultural minds America has ever known.

He had every reason to give up. But instead, he spent his life searching for ways to restore the soil that farming during American slavery had drained dry. He took the peanut—a crop no one saw value in—and found over 300 different uses for it.

He didn't just experiment with crops—he restored soil that slavery had drained. He took the overlooked peanut and turned it into over 300 products: oils, ink, paint, fuel, glue, cosmetics.

But most importantly, he taught poor Black farmers how to how to transform their condition and use what they already had to escape poverty.

He didn't hand out band-aids.

He handed out *blueprints*. He taught strategy. He built tools for liberation.

That's what culturally relevant tools do.
They don't just teach you to behave. They teach you how to build. Not just worksheets and curriculum. But systems, stories, and strategies built from the inside out—designed to restore what oppression stripped away.

## The Real Story Behind *Live Above the Hype*

You may or may not know that I wrote and developed a student life skills curriculum called "Live Above the Hype." It's a curriculum that guides young people to critically think about their own thought process, decision making and life outcomes and the influence their surrounding culture has on each of them. Thankfully this curriculum has made impact on thousands of students over the years. But let me take you to the beginning.

At the time of writing Live Above the Hype, I was a fairly young man, unfortunately, still living with the internalized belief that maybe I wouldn't live very long. That's what trauma-organized culture does—it normalizes early death.

So I thought: *Let me write a guidebook for my 7-year-old son, just in case I'm not here to teach him about life.*
But then I stopped myself. I'm not going anywhere. My son has me to guide him.

But many of the incarcerated young men I worked with had no one.

They were brilliant. Passionate. Misunderstood.
And the systems around them were not giving them what they needed.
So I said, *I'm going to build something for them.*
Not another bland "Just Say No" type book of rhetoric.
Not another program disconnected from their reality.
But a culturally rooted, emotionally intelligent, socially relevant curriculum—something they could see themselves in.
Something that didn't talk down to them... but called them *up.*

As I began writing the *book* it became more than a guide—it became a curriculum.
A reflective, conversation-based, culturally-grounded set of lessons pulled from my lived experiences and real interactions and conversations I'd had with the youth.

I wrote it like I talk. I wrote it to sound like *us.*
I included lessons I had taught, arguments I had mediated, and inner-battles I had watched unfold behind the eyes of young kings-in-training.

I knew I wouldn't always be as culturally relevant with the young people. One day, I would be the less cool, less relatable old guy.

So I documented my approach while it was still somewhat youthful—before the wisdom got lost.

I layered it with allegories, self-reflection questions, and identity-centered narratives.

But it was deeper than "teaching life skills."
It was about transforming how young people make decisions by helping them understand what they value.
I began writing from the understanding that behavior is driven by values.

See most life skills programs talk about behavior.
*Live Above the Hype* talks about values.
And too many youth are living out values they didn't choose for themselves—values that were handed to them by trauma, peer pressure, or distorted cultural norms.

So I built a tool that asks:

→ Is what you say you value really what you value?

→ Why do you value what you value?

→ Is it truly yours—or inherited from your environment?

→ Are your habits aligned with that value—or taking you further from it?

I took an almost anthropological approach to this work. I observed. I listened. I asked hard questions. And then I gave youth the language to challenge the "hype"—that hollow version of success we've been sold through media and trauma. The hype that says success and power is only found through destruction-mainly self destruction.

I called this curriculum *Live Above the Hype* because that's what we needed to do.
We needed to rise above the lies—
The lie that our worth is tied to destruction.
The lie that reputation is more important than life. The lie that success means losing your morals.

This wasn't just a curriculum.
It was a cultural intervention.

But let's be clear: I didn't create *Live Above the Hype* because I had extra time on my hands and needed an extra project to help kill a few hours in my day. I created it because what was already in place *wasn't working.*
How can we expect a young man who's dodging gang beef, grief, poverty, and institutional trauma to sit and

thrive in a classroom that never once acknowledges his reality?
How can a community be drug and gang impacted for 40+ years, and the curriculum never mentions how to navigate that reality?
That's malpractice.

## The Pushback: "Who's Going to Teach It?"

The early days were rough.

I was a younger man back then, knocking on every door I could.
I met with superintendents, curriculum directors—even the Superintendent of the State and his team.
I had no big-name institution behind me. No endorsements. Just vision, passion and truth.

They all loved the concept.
People would hear my presentation and say,
*"Wow. This is powerful."*
Then the question would come:
"But who's going to teach it?"

That question used to make me hotter than fish grease!
I would think to myself, "You mean to tell me your entire district is filled with trained educators, yet you can't find one person with enough cultural relevancy to teach a fully developed curriculum to your students? No one who knows how to connect with these kids?"
I realized that they weren't just asking a question. They were making a confession—
A confession that our education system was out of touch and doesn't reflect the youth it serves. I thought "yeah, I could teach it but that's not scalable. I could only be at so many places. And the vision was to impact the entire educational system."

Despite the constant discouragement... I kept going. And I wasn't willing to water down my work to get a "yes."

Gatekeepers continued to pass me off to someone else. So called advocates ignored my emails. Many powerful and influential people who could've opened important doors—but didn't. They would give me applause with no tangible support.

## The Breakthroughs

Eventually, persistence paid off.
I got a foot in the door at a youth detention facility. They said yes—to *one* session.
That turned into two... then into months. The young men took to it instantly.

I had young men who were rivals in the streets working together in my class.
I had boys who said the word "love" for the first time since childhood.
I even had a young man requesting to stay past his release date just to finish program and receive his high school diploma! Hard to believe but it's true. This may also be a clue to what his reality was like outside of jail. I still have the letter he wrote me:

*"I feel like I'm worth more than dying over a gang or over a street reputation... If you shut down the program, you will destroy kids who can achieve greatness."*

I also was able to get Live Above the Hype implemented in youth workforce development programs and alternative schools.

And now?
It's in school districts, youth detention centers, reentry

programs, alternative schools, and more all across the country.
Since 2014, we've been planting seeds in the places most people overlook.

## When You Teach the Tools Right, Everything Shifts

Every time this curriculum is implemented with integrity—not just as content, but as culture—it shifts something.

Staff say students start showing emotional intelligence. Conflicts go down. Self-respect goes up. The room feels different.

Because the tool works—but only when the foundation has been laid.

This is why we don't start here in the L.I.G.H.T. Model.
We end here. After the lens has been developed.
After identity has been inspired.
After growth has been guided.
After pain has been seen and acknowledged.

Then—and only then—can the tool take root.

## Tools, Timing, and the Power of Preparation

Imagine someone hands you a GPS and says,
"Here—you'll need this."
But they never help you define your destination.
Never teach you how to navigate obstacles.
Never even show you how to turn it on. Now the tool becomes a burden.
It makes you feel dumb. Frustrated. Ashamed.
You throw it away.

That's what happens when we give kids conflict resolution tools without first helping them build self-awareness.

Or when we give them "accountability checklists" but never guide them through healing from the things that made them numb in the first place.

This is also what happens when we give staff another curriculum to teach or program to facilitate without equipping them with the proper perspective, context or approach.

A tool is only powerful when it's connected to a purpose. Otherwise, it's just noise.

*"Don't hand them a tool until you've helped them believe they can build something."*

## What Legacy Really Means

*Live Above the Hype* isn't just my curriculum.
It's part of my legacy.
It's how I chose to stop waiting for permission and create something the community needed. This chapter isn't about a product.
It's about a mindset. A movement.
A mission to build tools that speak the language of the people.

To every visionary reading this: You don't need permission to make an impact.
You don't need a bunch of *letters* behind your name to create something powerful.
You just need the courage to say, *"If it doesn't exist yet, I'll build it."*

# RESOURCE SECTION

*Teach the Tools – Practical Guide for Implementing Live Above the Hype*

## 1. First, Build the Culture

Before implementing *Live Above the Hype*, pause and reflect:

→ Have your staff been trained in the L.I.G.H.T. Model?

→ Are they equipped to see beyond behavior and recognize value conflicts?

→ Have they reflected on their own lens, identity, growth journey, and emotional fatigue?

**Tools don't work in toxic soil.**
This curriculum thrives in environments where emotional safety, respect, and cultural authenticity are part of the daily air.

## 2. Overview of *Live Above the Hype*

**Purpose**:
A culturally responsive, emotionally intelligent life skills curriculum designed for youth impacted by systemic inequity, street culture, incarceration, and trauma.

**Core Pillars:**

→ Critical Thinking

→ Healthy Decision Making

→ Goal Setting & Achievement

→ Authentic Self-Identity

→ Self-Regulation

→ Positive Interpersonal Relationships

**Best For:**

→ Incarcerated youth

→ Youth in alternative schools

→ Reentry programs

→ Gang-impacted communities

→ Culturally disconnected school environments

**Format:**

→ Written in youth-accessible language

→ Infused with metaphors, questions, and culture-rooted examples

→ Built for real conversations, not textbook lectures

→ Flexible for 1:1 mentoring, group facilitation, or classroom adaptation

## 3. Sample Module Breakdown

Here's how one session might look:

**Module Theme:** *"You Say You Want Success"*

**Objective**: To help students explore whether their daily habits and identity align with their definition of success—or a definition they inherited from peers, media, or trauma.

**Opening Prompt**: "What does success mean to you? And where did that definition come from?"

**Key Excerpt** *(read aloud or assigned)*: *"Many say they want success, but they chase destruction because destruction is what they've been taught to value. If your definition of success isn't yours, how will the path you take ever feel right?"*

## Discussion Questions:

→ What's one "value" you say is important—but your actions contradict?

→ Is that value really yours, or did it come from your environment?

→ What does it look like to "Live Above the Hype" in this season of your life?

**Activity**: Have students draw two circles:

→ In Circle 1, list everything they say they value.

→ In Circle 2, list their daily actions/habits.
Then draw lines connecting which values and habits align—and which don't.

**Closing Reflection**: "Living above the hype means seeing through the lie and choosing the truth—even when it costs."


## 4. Facilitator Tips: How to Lead LATH Effectively

→ Don't lecture—facilitate.
Ask open-ended questions, sit in the silence, and let students process out loud.

→ Honor contradictions without shaming.
When students express conflicting values and actions, help them unpack why—don't shame them for inconsistency.

→ Use personal testimony wisely.
Only share when it helps center their story, not yours.

→ Keep the "why" visible.
Frequently remind youth that these lessons are for them, not to fix them.

→ Let tension lead to insight.
Disagreements, resistance, or emotional reactions are opportunities for reflection, not interruptions.

## 5. Curriculum Integration Models

Here are a few proven ways *Live Above the Hype* has been successfully implemented:

### School-Wide Advisory Program

→ Weekly 45-minute sessions during advisory/homeroom

→ Taught by trained teachers or designated SEL staff

→ Supports school culture, discipline reduction, and relational accountability

### Juvenile Detention Group

→ 60–90 minute small group sessions

→ Led by culturally fluent facilitators or external contractors

→ Youth create personal commitment statements after each section

## Reentry Program (Ages 18–26)

➜ 2-hour biweekly sessions

➜ Adapted for real-world application (employment, relationships, identity work)

➜ Blended with coaching and workforce development

## Train-the-Trainer Model

➜ Staff undergo multi-day professional development

➜ Equipped to facilitate curriculum internally with fidelity and cultural relevance

➜ Includes reflection journals, video examples, and peer feedback sessions

# 6. Implementation Tools

Here are a few simple tools to support effective rollout:

| TOOL | PURPOSE | HOW TO USE |
| --- | --- | --- |
| **Student Reflection Journal** | Capture insights and track emotional growth | After each session, students write responses to 2–3 key questions |
| **Value Alignment Map** | Connect values to actions | Visual tool students fill out each quarter to evaluate integrity |
| **Success Commitment Statement** | Translate goals into public accountability | Students share a commitment with peers or staff monthly |
| **Cultural Reflection Questions** | Make it real for students | "How does this show up in your neighborhood/family/music/etc.?" |

| TOOL | PURPOSE | HOW TO USE |
| --- | --- | --- |
| **Monthly Staff Circle** | Maintain emotional safety for facilitators | Staff come together for 45-minute reflection on their own lens and leadership |

## 7. Common Challenges & Coaching Scripts

### Challenge: "My students shut down when we talk about values."

**Try This**: "Sometimes we were never taught to think about what *we* value—only what we're supposed to value. That's why this feels awkward. And that's okay. This isn't about having the 'right' answer. It's about finally hearing your own voice."

### Challenge: "Some students resist every question like it's a setup."

**Try This**: "I'm not here to judge your answer. I'm here to help you slow down your thinking enough to know why you do what you do. That's where real power is."

### Challenge: "Staff struggle with staying emotionally regulated during resistance."

**Try This** (Internal Self-Check):

→ "Am I trying to control this moment—or connect through it?"

→ "What might this behavior be protecting them from?"

→ "How do I show up as a calm mirror—not a matching flame?"

# 8. What Makes *Live Above the Hype* Transformational?

Unlike other SEL or life skills programs, this curriculum:

→ Was created within the culture, not from outside of it

→ Tackles identity, environment, and value systems before "behavior"

→ Respects youth as thinkers, not projects

→ Helps staff transform with students—not just "manage" them

→ Was built by a practitioner who lived it—not just studied it

## Final Word to the Implementer:

Don't water it down. Don't rush through it.
And don't underestimate the brilliance in front of you.
Teach the tools, but remember: You are one of the tools.
Your presence, your story, your emotional regulation,
your ability to guide—not just instruct—is the greatest
curriculum your students will ever experience.

# CHAPTER 6

# SYSTEMS DON'T TRANSFORM UNTIL MINDSETS DO

*We don't have a training problem. We have a transformation problem.*

You can't shift culture with checklists. You can't build trust with top-down compliance. And you can't heal the hurt in our schools with frameworks that weren't built for the wounds we carry.

Yet that's exactly what's happening—across many school districts, reentry programs, youth systems, and workforce development programs that claim to serve the most vulnerable populations, but remain out of sync with the actual lives, pain, and brilliance of the people in them. Millions have been invested into programs. But what good is a program when the mindset behind it stays the same?

## The Cultural Gap That Keeps Recycling Failure

Let's name the reality we're in regarding youth:

→ A post-Crack (cocaine) era society

- → Living in a current opioid epidemic
- → Culture impacted by 40+ years of consistent gang turbulence
- → Still recovering from the impact of mass incarceration
- → A music industry that often normalizes and monetizes self-destructive narratives
- → A culture saturated with normalized sexual commodification
- → Navigating a social-media-driven, AI-fueled, uncertain economy

And we're still asking students to act like this doesn't affect them. Still asking teachers to "just teach the content" like context doesn't matter.
Still building classrooms that are emotionally blind and culturally tone-deaf.

This isn't about blame — it's about clarity. Because if we can't name the ecosystem that shapes our youth, we can't design systems that truly serve them.

Social Emotional Learning is no longer a cool elective to boost credits. It's a necessity.
And if staff haven't been equipped with the identity, empathy, and cultural readiness to *see the world their students come from*—any tool you hand them will get misused or rejected.

We don't just need curriculum.
We need recalibration.

## Systems That Say "Yes" But Think "No"

Let's talk about the lie of system support. I've sat across from district leaders, heads of departments, city program directors—even State Leaders of Education. This was years ago before concepts like trauma-informed practices and social emotional learning was getting the attention it's getting now. I was younger, less polished, but deeply passionate, and somewhat prepared. I brought the vision. I brought the work. I showed them the Live Above the Hype curriculum—life skills content that speaks directly to the identity, values, and social pressures our youth are navigating. I didn't ask for favors. I presented solutions.

They nodded. They smiled.
Some even clapped.

But then came *the* question.
*"We love it. But... who's going to teach it?"*

That question broke something in me.

Not because I didn't have an answer. But because it revealed everything that was broken in them. These are people tasked with educating and developing our youth—and they're telling me they don't know who on staff is equipped to teach social emotional learning to kids? Or when or where it they will have time to teach it?

We've built entire systems with staff who know their subject—but not their students.
Staff who can explain a standard—but can't connect to a struggle.
Staff who can recite policy—but can't speak to pain.
Systems don't fail because we lack tools.
They fail because we lack the mindset to effectively use them.

## The Breakthrough Baltimore Moment

For years, I fought to be heard.

My curriculum wasn't backed by a national nonprofit or elite university.
I didn't have celebrity endorsement, a grant-funded research team, or a PR campaign.

What I had was *proof*—years of real results in detention centers, school sites, and with youth that other people couldn't reach.

But still, I was often overlooked.
Educational "gatekeepers" gave compliments with no commitments.
Social justice advocates stayed silent.
Celebrities with power to open doors chose to keep theirs closed.

But I didn't wait for permission. I kept showing up.

As I was working nonstop in Southern California, a close friend of mine was advocating for the curriculum in the city of Baltimore. She saw the need. She believed in the work. And she committed to the cause. Then finally, through much of her efforts and a chain of connection, which included a former NFL player, a local pastor, and a community who was tired of waiting, an entire church congregation raised the funds to bring me to the city.

That led to professional development sessions across Baltimore.
Which led to Live Above the Hype being implemented in schools in the district.
This led to young men with no previous interest in education suddenly writing reflections, setting goals, and rebuilding their sense of self.

That wasn't just a win for me. It was a win for every visionary, every creative, every community-rooted educator who's been told they're "too passionate," "not academic enough," or "not the right fit" for the systems they're trying to impact.

## Don't Just Change the Paint. Reinforce the Foundation.

Imagine a school as a building. Every time test scores drop, or fights break out, someone suggests "a new paint job"—a fresh curriculum, a new policy, a new leader.

But if the foundation of that building is cracked—no amount of fresh paint will fix it.

## Mindset is the foundation.

- → If a teacher believes compliance equals respect, they'll confuse silence for safety.

- → If an administrator believes control equals culture, they'll miss the root of every outburst.

- → If a district only funds what's already validated, they'll never make space for what's deeply needed.

We keep trying to change outcomes without shifting beliefs.
We keep painting walls while ignoring the mold underneath.
We keep looking for surface-level solutions to soul-level problems.

You don't heal trauma with technique alone.
You address it with truth—and truth requires a mindset that's willing to see.

## You can't transform a system that still thinks the way the old one did.

This is why the L.I.G.H.T. Model doesn't start with tools. It starts with lens. With identity. With healing. With trust. Because once those things are *active*, the tools finally work.

In the final chapter, we'll bring everything full circle.

Let's talk about what it takes to build a L.I.G.H.T.-led culture—not just in one classroom, or one program, but
across schools, departments, agencies, and entire cities.

It's time to architect a new culture. One that was *built* for
this moment—and built for us.

# RESOURCE SECTION

*From Mindset to System Shift*

## MINDSET SHIFT CHECKLIST

Use this to assess if your current environment is operating from transformation—or tradition.

### If your system prioritizes...

| Traditional Mindset | Transformational Mindset |
| --- | --- |
| Compliance | Connection |
| Control | Collaboration |
| Standardized curriculum | Culturally-rooted learning |
| "What works on paper" | "What works in real life" |
| Avoiding risk | Embracing relevance |
| Data as the only proof | Dignity as part of the outcome |
| Discipline first | Healing first |

**Reflection Prompt:**
Which 2–3 traditional mindsets do you see most in your environment?

_______________________________________

_______________________________________

_______________________________________

What's the cost of leaving them unchallenged?

_______________________________________________

_______________________________________________

_______________________________________________

# SYSTEM-SHIFTING STRATEGIES FOR LEADERS

Here are bold, practical strategies to embed transformation into your system—not just your training.

## 1. Reframe "Professionalism"

Too often, systems define professionalism through outdated norms.

Redefine it to include:

- Emotional self-regulation
- Cultural responsiveness
- Community fluency
- Ability to connect and redirect without shame

## 2. Normalize "Cultural Humility" in Hiring & PD

Make it part of your staff development process to ask:

- How does your background impact how you see the youth we serve?
- What biases are you actively unlearning?
- When was the last time you relearned what's relevant to the population you serve?

## 3. Create a Culturally Responsive Curriculum Task Force

Form a diverse internal team (youth included) to review:

→ How culturally relevant your current curriculum is

→ What life skills are currently taught—and what's missing

→ What social norms your school reinforces (explicitly or by default)

## 4. Fund Solutions Led by Lived Experience

If a curriculum or program was created by someone from the community—don't ask "where's the data?" before you ask "how can we support this?"

# SYSTEM MINDSET SELF-INQUIRY

Use these prompts in staff meetings, PD sessions, or team retreats.

## For Individuals:

→ What mindsets about youth behavior did I inherit that no longer serve our mission?

→ What do I assume is "just how it is" that may actually be a policy choice, not a necessity?

→ When have I seen a youth transform—and what made it possible?

## For Teams:

→ Where does our system show more fear of disruption than commitment to change?

→ What do we fund that we don't even believe in anymore?

→ What's something we keep saying "we can't do" that we've actually never really tried?

## MINDSET-LED POLICY EXAMPLES

Transformational systems don't just use better language—they build better structures.

| Old Policy | Rewritten with a Mindset Shift |
| --- | --- |
| "Zero Tolerance" | "Restorative Accountabllity" |
| "Suspension for Disrespect" | "Intervention for Emotional Dysregulation" |
| "No cell phones allowed" | "Guided Tech Use & Digital Literacy" |
| "No talking during class" | "Community agreements about engagement" |

## FORWARD-THINKING ACTIONS FOR EXECUTIVE LEADERS

Use this as your *next steps* roadmap to begin shifting culture today.

### Immediate (This Month)

→ Host a team reflection using the Mindset Shift Checklist

→ Identify 1–2 outdated practices your team is ready to retire

→ Invite a community-rooted leader to review your SEL curriculum

### Short-Term (Next 90 Days)

→ Launch an internal "Cultural Fluency" PD Series

→ Pilot Live Above the Hype curriculum at one site

→ Allocate budget toward lived-experience-based programs

## Long-Term (6–12 Months)

→ Restructure onboarding to include trauma-informed, culturally responsive approaches

→ Develop a youth advisory board that informs engagement strategy

→ Rework your definition of success to include student voice, dignity, and emotional safety

## REAL TALK SCRIPT: WHEN PUSHBACK HITS

When leadership or staff says: "We don't have time for this social-emotional stuff."

You can respond with: "Then we're not preparing students for life—we're just preparing them for testing. And the world tests their identity every single day."

## FINAL REFLECTION:

**Systems don't transform until mindsets do—because the system is just a reflection of who's in charge, what they believe, and what they fear.**

# CHAPTER 7

# BUILD THE CULTURE

*Why healthy environments don't happen by accident—and how to build one with intention, consistency, and soul.*

**W**hat we tolerate is what we teach.
*What we model is what they mirror.*
*What we avoid becomes culture by default.*

By the time you reach this chapter, you've already been equipped with the mindset, the lens, the identity-building strategies, the growth-guiding tools, and the healing-centered frameworks that make youth engagement sustainable.

But here's the truth most systems skip over:

Culture is where the real transformation lives—or dies. And not just youth culture. Staff culture. Leadership culture. Institutional culture. Because you can have the right curriculum, the right mission statement, the right training—and still watch a system fail if the culture underneath it contradicts the values you're trying to teach. So, let's start with clarity.

## What Is Culture?

In youth-serving environments, *culture* is not just your rules, your dress code, or your student handbook.

Culture is the *unwritten but deeply felt rhythm* of a space. It's what people believe is normal, tolerated, expected, or rewarded.

It's the *emotional tone* of your environment. If climate is the weather of the day, culture is the atmosphere that holds it all together.

In an organization, culture is shaped by many forces:

- People and leadership
- Structure and processes
- Technology and policies
- External influences
- Incentives and accountability

But ultimately, culture is the shared interpretation of *"what is and why it is."*
And in youth settings, this becomes personal—fast.

## The Core Truth

You can't just teach values. You have to *build environments* that breathe them.

One solid mentor can change a life. But a solid culture? That can change a generation.

A positive classroom climate is a good start.
But a culture is what youth begin to carry with them, even after the program ends. It's the difference between having a "cool staff member" and having a collective standard.

Between isolated inspiration and community transformation.

## Culture Is What Gets Reinforced—Not What Gets Said

You can write respect on a poster. You can frame it in a mission statement. But if students see that disrespect gets attention, validation, or fear-based obedience, then disrespect becomes the real culture.

Culture is built in:

→ The way you greet a student after they come back from suspension.

→ What happens when someone gets it wrong—not just when they get it right.

→ The consistent energy students feel from you even when they're not showing up right.

Culture is created by repetition. Repetition creates rhythm. Rhythm builds memory. Memory becomes identity.

### *Classroom as a Barbershop*

If you've ever been in a real community barbershop, you know:

It's not just about haircuts. It's about tone, ritual, and energy. There's a rhythm to it. There are unspoken rules about how to act, how to connect, how to respect the space. That's culture.

Same with the classroom. Or a youth program. It's not just about the curriculum. It's the tone that's set, the way people are treated, the standards people rise to, and the love that holds it all together.

## Culture-Building Isn't Just About Youth—It's About Staff, Too

Too many leaders try to fix youth culture...without ever addressing the adult culture that influences the conditions. We can't build youth accountability if we don't model adult accountability. We can't expect emotional maturity from youth if staff are still leading from unhealed frustration, ego, or superiority. Culture is not about controlling behavior. It's about shaping belief systems through the experiences people consistently have in your space. If your space doesn't feel safe, it won't feel sacred. And what's not sacred won't be respected.

Culture Killers to Watch For

- "That's not my job" energy from staff
- Gossip as connection between adults
- Favoritism disguised as mentorship
- Public shaming as behavior correction
- Zero transparency from leadership
- Cynicism masked as realism
- Youth constantly being told to "be leaders" in spaces where adults don't lead by example

## How to Begin Shaping the Culture (Even If You're Not the Boss)

Influencing culture doesn't require a title. It requires a decision. Start small. Start consistent. Start now. Ask yourself:

- What energy do I bring when I enter the room?
- What is my "emotional tone" setting for the space?
- What do I reinforce—directly or indirectly?
- What do I ignore that sends a silent message?

You don't need permission to raise the standard. You just need alignment, clarity, and consistency.

## Signs You're Building a Transformational Culture

You know you're shifting the culture when:

→ Respect isn't a reward—it's a reflex.

→ Youth challenge each other with maturity, not mockery.

→ Staff stop avoiding hard conversations and start holding each other accountable—with care.

You'll hear fewer power struggles—and more real questions. You'll see:

→ Youth lifting each other up instead of tearing each other down

→ Staff addressing harm in real time instead of sweeping it under the rug

→ Emotional safety replacing toxic silence

You'll *feel*:

→ A presence of trust

→ A pattern of respect

→ A culture of connection

## A Healthy Culture Is Like the Immune System

A healthy culture is self-regulating. It *protects* the environment from toxic behavior—and *welcomes* people who want to heal and grow.

Like a human immune system, a healthy culture:

→ Fights off viruses (toxicity, sabotage, unchecked trauma)

- → Supports the healing of injuries (conflict, breakdown, betrayal)

- → Recognizes when something doesn't belong—and when something needs more support to grow

But here's the catch:

A toxic culture can attack the cure. A broken culture can reject the people who are *trying to fix it*. That's why culture work must be *intentional*, *communal*, and *led by example*.

## When Youth Shape the Culture

Let me tell you a real story. I was called into a school in a youth detention center where the environment had become combative, toxic, and deeply divided. Staff were frustrated. Students were shut down or explosive. Nobody trusted anybody.

They brought me in to "help shift the culture." But instead of just leading a training, I asked to hold a *gathering*. I told leadership: "I need everyone in the room: Youth (the leaders), teachers, youth correctional officers, a couple school administrators, and the top leadership of the detention center"—what some would call the warden.

We gathered in what is called a restorative leadership circle—though we weren't in a circle at all. I started by asking the youth:
*"What's not working here? What do you need to say that's never been heard?"*

The youth spoke up with passion, frustration, and honesty. After they finished speaking,
one of the top leaders of the facility (the warden)
responded. As he began to speak, a student interrupted him with intensity. The moment was tense.

I immediately intervened and told the student: "Listen... You have the attention of a decision-maker, who did not have to be here. He chose to be here. Don't blow this moment. You should be listening because he is responding specifically to what you just said. You're not just speaking for yourself right now—you're opening the door for every young person in this system to be heard. Let's keep it respectful."

That student nodded and began to quietly listen. The room shifted.

We kept going with our meeting, listening to each other with the intent to understand. The culture began to balance in real time. After the meeting the warden said he had never experienced anything like that with the "inmates" (which is what he called them). He shared how amazing that session was and said he wanted me to come back to work with his correctional officers. We exchanged information and said we would talk soon.

After that day, I flew back home to California. In the weeks that followed, I kept hearing:

"Fights are way down."

"Students are listening."

"There's a different vibe in the building."

Students were checking each other respectfully and holding each other accountable, saying things like, "Nah, we not doing that no more."
"We gotta *live above the hype*." It was a great victory.

But unfortunately, when culture change isn't consistently modeled, reinforced, and protected—old habits return. I never got a return call from the warden. The school became too busy to continue our in person follow sessions. And eventually, because the leadership didn't follow through with sustained support, the culture slid back into dysfunction—and I was called in again months later to do some mentoring workshops with the students.

That's how fragile culture is. And that's how powerful youth voice can be—if we don't waste it.

## Staff Culture Influences Youth Culture

The way staff treat each other is often the *real curriculum* students absorb.

If your adult team models:

- Avoidance
- Gossip
- Power trips
- Passive-aggression
- Inconsistent expectations

...then don't be surprised when youth mirror those exact behaviors.

But if staff model:

- Mutual respect
- Emotional accountability
- Clear boundaries
- Collective ownership
- Celebration of growth

...then youth start to embody those values too. You don't get culture change through a one-off assembly. You build it by living it in every hallway, every meeting, every moment.

## The Most Common Mistake in Culture Work

Too many leaders try to change the culture from the outside in. They create new policies, hire a new consultant, or bring in a one-time speaker—but they never involve the people most affected by the culture.

*Compliance without connection is just a countdown to collapse.* If your culture shift doesn't feel like a win for the staff *and* the students...
If there's no room for reflection, voice, or ownership...
It's not transformation. It's just temporary control.

## The Mantra That Keeps Me Grounded

When resistance is high and change is slow, I remind myself:

*"I represent the mission, not my ego."*

I don't need to be the loudest in the room.
I don't need to win every battle.
I just need to make sure the mission keeps moving forward.

That's what building culture really means:
Creating a space where the mission is felt, lived, and passed on—even when you're not in the room.

## A Word to Leaders

You can't build a youth culture of empowerment with an adult culture of dysfunction.

You can't tell youth to live above the hype if your staff are stuck beneath it.

And you can't ask students to transform unless you're willing to model what transformation looks like. Culture is not delegated. Its modeled— or muted. If your staff sees that you tolerate toxicity in the name of "experience" or "seniority," they will start believing that consistency is optional, and accountability is political. If you want a culture rooted in *dignity*, *transparency*, *connection*, and *healing*—you model it first. Your posture becomes the policy.

Curriculum shapes what we teach.
Relationships shape how we reach.
But culture shapes who we become together.
If the culture isn't right, no curriculum can make it work.

**Curious how your culture scores?**
*Scan here for your free AI Culture Stability Diagnostic.*

# RESOURCE SECTION

*Tools for Cultural Transformation*

**"Culture doesn't happen just by talking about it—it happens by living it."**

Below are tools, scripts, prompts, and protocols to help youth professionals build healthy, healing-centered environments with intentionality, strategy, and soul.

## 1. Staff Culture Alignment Exercise: "What We Model Is What They Mirror"

**Purpose:** Build adult alignment before expecting youth alignment.

**Instructions (Staff Session – 45 minutes):**

1. Split into small groups.
2. Reflect and write your answers to the following:

   → What are 3 behaviors we consistently model as staff?
   → What are 3 behaviors we avoid addressing (but know we should)?
   → What messages might youth be absorbing from our adult interactions?

3. Regroup for a full-team dialogue:

    → What's one cultural behavior we want to double down on?
    → What's one behavior we need to disrupt as a staff?

4. Close by writing a team agreement:
   *"In order to build a culture rooted in respect, healing, and consistency, we agree to..."*

Follow-Up Tip: Post the team agreement in staff common areas—and revisit monthly.

## 2. Youth Voice Prompts: "Culture Through Their Eyes"

Use these prompts in advisory circles, journaling, or leadership workshops to center youth experiences and gather insight.

### Prompt Options:

→ "What makes you feel respected by adults in this space?"

→ "What unspoken rules do students follow here that adults don't notice?"

→ "If you could change one thing about how people are treated in this space, what would it be?"

→ "What do you think the 'real culture' of this school/program is?"

→ "What does 'Living Above the Hype' mean to you in how we treat each other?"

> **Pro Tip:** Don't just collect responses—respond to them. Share back what you heard. Co-create solutions where appropriate.

# 3. Culture Pulse Checklist (Walkthrough Tool)

**Use this tool to observe and assess the culture of your school, program, or organization.**

| Observation Category | Key Indicators | Yes / No / Notes |
| --- | --- | --- |
| **Emotional Tone** | Youth and staff greet each other warmly | |
| | Humor, joy, or encouragement are visible | |
| | Adults de-escalate, not inflame, conflict | |
| **Communication** | Staff communicate clearly and consistently | |
| | Youth voice is invited and acknowledged | |
| | Staff avoid public shaming or sarcasm | |
| **Accountability** | Harm is addressed in the moment (not avoided) | |
| | Consequences are fair, transparent, and restorative | |
| | Staff hold each other accountable with care | |
| **Youth Ownership** | Youth take initiative to redirect peers | |
| | Youth identify with cultural values (e.g. "Live Above the Hype") | |
| | Youth leadership roles are visible and respected | |

Use this checklist monthly to reflect on what's growing—and what needs repair.

## 4. 10-Minute Staff Huddle Protocol (Weekly Culture Tune-Up)

**Why:** Culture erodes in silence. A quick rhythm of reflection builds alignment.

**When:** Weekly (Fridays or Mondays recommended)
**Duration:** 10–15 minutes
**Facilitator:** Rotates weekly (empowers different voices)

### Flow:

1. **Anchor Quote (1 min):** Open with a quote about youth, leadership, or culture.

2. **Highlight (2 min):** One example of someone living the culture well.

3. **One Shift (5 min):** What's one small culture adjustment we can make this week?

4. **Youth Voice (2 min):** Share a student quote or reflection that challenges or inspires us.

5. **Close (2 min):** Name an intention for the week (e.g., "This week I'll lead with patience.")

## 5. Culture Re-Alignment Script: When Things Slip

**Scenario:** You notice the culture shifting back into old, toxic, or unaligned behaviors.

Use this script to refocus the team without shame or blame.

**Script:**
*"I want to take a quick pause—not to call anyone out, but to call us back into alignment. We've done too much good work to let the culture slip. Let's remind ourselves: what we tolerate becomes the culture. I know we're all*

*under pressure, but our students feel what we model. Let's name what needs to shift and commit to course-correcting—together."*

Then ask:

→ "What have we been tolerating that we shouldn't?"

→ "What's one culture standard we need to re-commit to?"

# 6. Restorative Circle Planning Tool: Youth-Adult Culture Reset

Use this when rebuilding trust, repairing harm, or re-establishing norms.

**Participants:** Students + Staff
**Preparation:** Choose 3–5 youth and 3–5 staff representatives

## Circle Format:

1. **Opening Round (1 word check-in)**

2. **Youth Question:** "What do you want staff to understand about what it's like being a student here?"

3. **Staff Question:** "What do you wish students knew about the pressure of supporting this environment?"

4. **Shared Question:** "What would it look like to build a space we're all proud of?"

5. **Commitment Round:** Each person names one commitment to help shift the culture

**Close with a unifying phrase**, like:
*"We don't need perfection. We need partnership."*
*"We don't just work here. We shape here."*
*"We are the culture."*

## 7. Culture Identity Mapping Activity (Youth + Staff)

**Goal:** Identify the current "cultural identity" of your space—and reimagine what it could be.

**Instructions:**
Create two columns:

→ Column 1: "Our Current Culture…"

→ Column 2: "Our Ideal Culture…"

## Prompts:

→ "When someone walks in, what do they feel?"

→ "How do people resolve conflict?"

→ "What behaviors are rewarded vs ignored?"

→ "What's the emotional tone of our space?"

Have teams or classes fill it out, then create a visual mural or poster from the ideal vision.

## 8. Cultural Norms Reboot Tool: What We Say, What We Do

**Use this as a reflective group activity.**

| Posted Norm | How We Actually Practice It | Needed Shift |
| --- | --- | --- |
| "Respect Everyone" | Adults cut off youth when they're upset | Practice active listening before correcting |
| "Be Responsible" | Staff avoid accountability for missed meetings | Model accountability openly and positively |

| Posted Norm | How We Actually Practice It | Needed Shift |
| --- | --- | --- |
| "No Bullying" | Students constantly roast each other without pushback | Teach healthy humor vs. hurtful jokes |

Use in team meetings or youth town halls to make culture correction collaborative—not top-down.

## 9. Culture-Building Mantras for Adults (Post + Repeat)

Place these in staff rooms, emails, or meetings to keep the mindset alive.

→ "Culture is built by what we consistently allow—or don't."

→ "I don't need to control students. I need to create conditions for leadership."

→ "If I want them to care, I have to model care."

→ "We don't just run programs. We build ecosystems."

→ "What I do teaches louder than what I say."

## 10. Final Reminder: You Don't Need Permission to Build Culture

If you're waiting for someone else to give you the green light, here it is:

Lead the culture shift.
Name the standard.
Model the value.
Create what you wish existed.

The ecosystem transforms when individuals choose to live the culture they believe in—out loud and on purpose.

# CHAPTER 8

# INSTITUTIONALIZE THE TRANSFORMATION

## *From Inspiration to Infrastructure*

Think of the last time you left a conference, training, or keynote feeling unstoppable. The speaker's words lit a fire in you. You vowed to change the way you lead, teach, or show up for your youth.

Now think about two months later...

The fire? Dimmed. The new practices? Forgotten. The system around you? The same.

The truth is: inspiration can spark change, but only systems can sustain it. Culture shifts that *inspire* people are important — but unless they are embedded into the *structure* of how an organization operates, they fade. The difference is like hearing a motivational speech vs. participating in a hands-on training that retools your daily practice. One creates a spark. The other installs wiring that keeps the lights on permanently.

## The Core Message

Organizational transformation that lasts must be modeled by leadership, built into systems, and reinforced through incentives and accountability. Otherwise, it stays in the realm of temporary compliance rather than permanent change.

## Why Institutionalization Gets a Bad Reputation

Many resist "institutionalization" because they equate it with bureaucracy, control, or rigidity. And to be fair, some organizations have weaponized it that way — making abrupt, reactive changes without considering staff needs or readiness.

But real institutionalization isn't about control — it's about *embedding shared values into the bones of the system.*

When done poorly, change management:

→ Feels abrupt and reactionary

→ Is rolled out without consultation or communication

→ Damages morale and trust

→ Creates "us vs. them" between leadership and staff

When done well, change management:

→ Brings people along early and often

→ Clearly communicates the "why" and the benefits

→ Provides tools and support

→ Reinforces the change until it becomes second nature

## The Two Forms of Change

→ Planned Change – Deliberate, communicated, and resourced

→ Unplanned Change – Forced by unexpected events

Too often, leaders present a planned change as if it's unplanned — springing it on staff with no warning. This is where resistance happens.

## When Institutionalization Worked

Several years ago, I was called into a youth development program where emotional safety was a value on paper but not in practice. Staff agreed it was important, but there were no systems to ensure it happened daily.

We built "emotional safety" into:

→ Hiring Practices – Candidates were screened for empathy and youth-centered approaches.

→ Onboarding – Every new hire went through a training module on trauma-informed interaction.

→ Daily Routines – A 5-minute emotional climate check-in was added to all morning staff huddles.

Within six months, student incident reports dropped, and staff turnover decreased. The key wasn't just talking about safety — it was building it into the organization's operating system.

## Leadership's Role in Sustaining Transformation

Leaders must:

1. **Model the change** — visible alignment between words and actions.

2. **Communicate relentlessly** — repeat the "why" until it becomes part of the organizational DNA.

   → Once you start to paint the picture and explain WHY things are changing, everyone begins to understand the long-term vision.

→ They want to be a part of the solution because they begin to form an emotional connection with the goals.

3. **Anticipate resistance** — and reframe change as an opportunity, not a threat.

4. **Make the new way easier than the old way** — through tools, processes, and incentives.

When leaders fail to model the values they promote, morale erodes, resentment grows, and credibility collapses.

# RESOURCE SECTION

## *Institutionalize the Transformation*

**Institutionalization Toolkit**

### 1. Change Readiness Checklist *(for Leaders)*

Before announcing any initiative, confirm:

→ We have clearly defined the desired change.

→ We have explained the "why" and tied it to our mission.

→ We have engaged key influencers early.

→ We have allocated resources (time, tools, training).

→ We have a reinforcement plan (recognition, incentives, follow-up).

### 2. Staff Communication Script for Change Rollouts

**Opening:** "I want to share a change we're implementing, why it matters, and how it will help us better serve our youth."
**Middle:** "Here's the benefit to you, our team, and the young people we serve. Here's what will stay the same, and here's what will be different."

**Close:** "I want to hear your thoughts and questions. This change will be successful if we all shape it together."

## 3. Change Impact Map

| | |
|---|---|
| **What's Changing** | e.g., "We're adding a daily emotional climate check-in." |
| **Impact on Staff** | e.g., "Extra 5 minutes at start of shift." |
| **Support Provided** | e.g., "Scripts and prompts for check-ins." |

## 4. Youth-Adult Partnership Protocol

➜ Include youth in at least one decision-making body.

➜ Create formal channels for youth feedback.

➜ Publicly show how youth input shapes decisions.

## 5. Embedding Change Into Systems

Embed the transformation into:

➜ Job descriptions

➜ Performance evaluations

➜ Staff onboarding

➜ Budget allocations

➜ Daily/weekly meeting agendas

## 6. Rituals That Reinforce the Change

➜ Monthly "culture pulse" meetings

➜ Quarterly recognition for living the values

➜ Yearly training refreshers

➜ Storytelling moments in staff meetings

# FINAL WORD

## *THE WORK BENEATH THE WORK*

Transformation doesn't end when the training concludes or when the last page is turned.
It begins again—every morning you walk through the door, every time a young person tests your patience, every moment you decide whether to react or to respond.

The truth is: the systems won't change just because you finished this book. They'll change because *you* decided to lead differently.

You've learned that culture isn't just a climate—it's a code. It's written and rewritten daily through what you reinforce, what you ignore, and what you model. And in youth-serving work, that code determines whether we reproduce trauma or rewrite legacy.

## The Responsibility of Leadership

Every generation inherits both the pain and the potential of the one before it.
But the leaders who change history are the ones who translate pain into process—
who take what they've learned in survival and convert it into structure.
That's what *institutionalizing transformation* really means.

It's not about more policies or programs.
It's about leaders who create safety, dignity, and accountability in how we work together.

## The Culture Keepers

Maybe you're a teacher in a classroom, a counselor in a reentry program, or a director running a youth initiative.
Whatever your role, you are a *culture keeper*.
Your presence communicates possibility.
Your consistency builds credibility.
Your integrity becomes the curriculum your team and your students learn from.

Remember: Transformation doesn't depend on charisma—it depends on consistency.
It's not about who talks the loudest, but who models the standard the longest.

## The Invitation

My hope is that this book gave you language for what your spirit already knew—that culture shapes everything. And that you have the authority to shape it.

The question now isn't "what will you do with this book?" It's *"what will this book do through you?"*

Because the real measure of this work isn't in the quotes you highlight. It's in the culture you build.
Every conversation. Every classroom. Every moment that tests your patience and reveals your purpose.

So keep building. Keep modeling. Keep transforming systems from within.
Because the world doesn't change through compliance—it changes through courage.
And your courage to build culture... is the curriculum.

# AUTHOR REFLECTION

I've walked through classrooms, community centers, and correctional facilities that taught me one truth: transformation is possible anywhere there's belief, consistency, and love with boundaries.

This book isn't just a reflection of what I've taught—it's the culmination of what I've learned from those who were once written off, but chose to rise anyway.

So wherever you lead, lead with light. Because when you change the way people experience leadership... you change what they believe is possible.

Lead With LIGHT
***K-Rahn Vallatine***

www.ingramcontent.com/pod-product-compliance
Lightning Source LLC
Chambersburg PA
CBHW021549150726
47990CB00006B/2469